If I Eat Another Carrot I'll Go Crazy

The Five Point Way to a Healthy Heart

Dr Ross G.T. Walker

KINGSCLEAR BOOKS

Kingsclear Books (ACN 001904034)

3/77 Willoughby Road, Crows Nest 2065

Phone (02) 9439 5093

Facsimile (02) 9439 0430

Copyright © Ross G.T. Walker 1996
Printed 1996, reprinted 1996, 1997, new edition 1998, reprinted 1999

ISBN 0-908272-43-X

Illustrations by Dennis Richards

Printed and bound by The Griffin Press Pty Ltd Australia

Dr Ross G.T. Walker MB BS (Hons.) FRACP

Dr Ross G.T. Walker is a cardiologist with a private practice at Hunters Hill. He specialises in echocardiology and preventative cardiology. He lectures on preventative cardiology to a wide range of groups in the community interested in health, diet and exercise. Dr Walker is in the process of establishing the first service in Australia for Electron Beam Tomography which is the most accurate method available for detecting heart disease in its early stages.

His training in echocardiology has been in the Prince Henry Hospital and Prince of Wales Hospital, Sydney; Prince Charles Hospital, Brisbane; the University of Bonn, Germany; the Thorax Centre, Rotterdam, Holland.

In 1994 Dr Walker was appointed to the Sydney Adventist Hospital to provide a comprehensive service in echocardiology. Having the largest cardiology department in New South Wales in the state's largest private hospital, this hospital employs 20 cardiologists and conducts 15 bypass procedures per week. Dr Walker also established the Baringa Cardiology Centre in Coffs Harbour on the north coast of New South Wales.

Dr Walker has lectured extensively on echocardiology and preventative cardiology throughout Australasia, Asia and North America. He is a sought after identity on the public speaking circuit and has a weekly health programme on 6PR in Perth. He also appears regularly with Dr James Wright, a prominent Sydney medical practitioner, as a guest on his radio programme discussing cardiac health and stress.

Acknowledgements

I would like to thank Dr Don Anderson, Macquarie Street cardiologist, for introducing me to the joys of clinical cardiology. Professor David Wilcken, Ralph Blackett and Dr Jean Palmer are acknowledged for initiating my interest in preventative cardiology. Professor David Colquhoun, my good friend, taught me the intricacies of the Mediterranean lifestyle. Barbara Lowery, the ABC food consultant, helped spark my interest in public speaking and introduced me to the food industry. Thanks to my dear friend, Dennis Richards, who did the drawings and whose talents will be recognised beyond this book. And finally, thanks to my lovely wife Anne and my five children, Paul, Alexandra, David, Bridget and Isabelle, without whom I would never achieve anything.

FOREWORD

Diseases of the circulation are the major killers in the world and account for approximately ten million deaths annually. Similar numbers of deaths occur in the developed and developing countries. By far the largest disease affecting the circulation is coronary heart disease. Coronary heart disease is not an inevitable consequence of aging but is one of the classic diseases of Western civilization. Coronary heart disease does not exist in hunter-gatherer communities and is rarely seen in communities with traditional simple diets or communities around the Mediterranean basin. As the developing countries improve their living standard, coronary heart disease is a looming problem.

The good news is that coronary heart disease is largely preventable with modification of lifestyle. Dr Ross Walker, a friend and colleague of mine, is a cardiologist with a passion for preventative medicine. We have spent many hours together discussing the benefits of a Mediterranean lifestyle and how this can be adapted to the Australian context. Ross's book is a natural extension of his enthusiasm and passion for this important subject. He has an engaging personal style which comes through in this informative and readable book. Western medicine has made enormous progress over the last decade or two, particularly in management of patients who have developed coronary heart disease. The long-term solution for the coronary heart disease epidemic is basic lifestyle changes.

Dr Walker has clearly set out a plan which is achievable, to change lifestyle and avoid the most common cause of death in our community. The lifestyle changes which Dr Walker recommends probably will also have a significant impact in decreasing the common cancers. Low fat diet plans are often too restrictive and compliance is usually poor in the long term. Ross Walker's way is enjoyable, life enhancing, and in a word, fun! I would encourage all readers to adopt the Walker Plan and reap the benefits of a richer, healthier and longer life.

Dr David Colquhoun MB, BS, FRACP

TABLE OF CONTENTS

Dedicated to Anne

CHAPTER 1

Five Case Studies
for the
Five Point Way

Case 1: The Asian Businessman

On Saturday morning, 17 January 1998, a prominent Asian businessman woke feeling unwell. Despite this, he went to the gym. He commented to the instructor that he was not feeling well. He then commenced his training. When he returned home he felt cold and tired and decided to sleep (something he never did at this time of day).

Three hours later he woke for his usual Saturday afternoon tennis match. He commented to his partner that he wasn't well. During the game he collapsed and was pronounced dead on arrival at hospital. An autopsy revealed he had died of severe coronary heart disease. He was only 42 years old. This man was thin and a fitness fanatic who ate all the right foods. Why did he die prematurely?

1

Case 2: The High Flier

In late 1993, I was referred a 53-year-old pilot for a cardiac risk assessment. He had no symptoms apart from the usual fatigue one would expect in a hard-working person with a responsible job. He had a ten year history of hypertension (high blood pressure) and a family history of premature death from coronary heart disease.

With new heart scanning techniques, I observed his heart was normal at rest, as was his cardiogram (recording of the changes in the rhythm of the heart). After 15 minutes of heavy exercise on standard computer exercise protocol he felt quite well but the test was stopped because of dramatic changes on his cardiograph. The repeat scan revealed that his heart, which was normal at rest, had almost stopped beating, despite the lack of symptoms. He was immediately referred for an angiogram (a dye study of the heart arteries). This revealed all three main arteries in his heart were blocked. He has since had coronary artery bypass surgery and has recovered very well. Why didn't he die with such severe disease? Why didn't he have any symptoms?

Case 3: The Heart Surgeon Needing His Own Medicine

Daniel is a 50 year old cardiac surgeon. He plays squash once a week, has a stressful life but, apart from feeling tired, is pretty fit. His cholesterol was normal (5.4 mmol/L or 210mg/dL), his blood pressure 120 over 80 and he hadn't smoked for 15 years. Both of his parents are still alive and in their eighties.

Daniel was visiting friends in San Francisco and had read in one of the prestigious cardiology journals about a new and extremely accurate test to predict future heart disease. This test, known as Electron Beam Tomography, scans through the

heart in around 30 seconds and photographs the coronary arteries. The scanner then measures the amount of calcium build up in the arteries. Calcium is an accurate marker for fat content. The computer then gives a score which indicates the absence or presence of coronary artery disease and its severity.

A zero score means no disease and a close to zero chance of developing any in the next five to ten years. A score of ten indicates mild disease, 100 is moderate disease and greater than 400 indicates severe fat build up throughout the arteries.

Daniel made an appointment at San Francisco Heart Scan to have his Electron Beam Tomography performed and you can imagine his shock when he was told his score was 907. Without this information Daniel would have been in severe trouble. He had a stress echo which was normal. He had a coronary angiogram that showed significant fat build up at the sites of heavy calcium shown on the EBT but as yet he had no major obstructions. This would only be a matter of time.

So how does Daniel have such a significant build up of fat in his arteries without any symptoms?

Case 4: James Fixx

At the age of 32 James Fixx had a heart attack. He was over-weight, smoked, ate the wrong foods and had high cholesterol. He realised that if he didn't change his ways, he was not long for this life. He completely changed his lifestyle and became world renowned for his book, *The Complete Book of Running*. At the age of 49 he developed chest pain. This was after 17 years of feeling well, with no symptoms. He mentioned his pain to his friends who said, 'It can't be too serious, you can run marathons without any problems!'

After six weeks of intermittent pain, James was to run in a race. On the morning of the race, he complained to a nurse that he had chest pain. The comment was made 'James, you're too fit to have any serious troubles.' James ran in the race, collapsed and died. James Fixx could run marathons, how could he possibly have died of heart problems? Why, after 17 years, did his disease finally catch up with him?

Case 5: The Construction Worker

Most perplexing is the case of a 76-year-old, retired construction worker. He has smoked since the age of 14, drinks too much alcohol and weighs 110 kilograms. This man hardly ever visits a doctor.

The last time he was in hospital was at the age of five to have his tonsils removed. Despite his horrendous lifestyle and lack of concern for himself, He has survived, against all odds! Why hasn't he had any heart problems? What has protected him?

The first four cases are very different presentations of coronary heart disease, still the biggest killer in the Western world and increasing at a rapid rate in Asia. The last case is a man who despite his lifestyle appears immune to coronary heart disease.

Why is this book different?

When you take a walk through any bookshop, you will see shelf after shelf of books on lifestyle: how to live longer, how to live better, how to eat properly, how to lose weight, how to put on weight, how not to worry, how to make more money, how to make less money. Why then do you need another book on lifestyle?

This book will give you the total picture of heart disease and how it is generated. It will give you simple and straightforward guidelines on what to do to prevent it. Let me say that there is no place in your life for diets or constant exercise. You need a moderate, global approach to your life with realistic advice, goals that are easy to achieve and some new and interesting concepts thrown in. As a cardiologist who sees patients with all types of heart disease, I would prefer to 'prevent the fire rather than have to put it out.'

When I started practising cardiology over twelve years ago, I was distressed to see people coming back to the hospital for their second or third coronary artery bypass operation. It was obvious to me that a bypass was only a temporary procedure, although many of the patients believed they were cured once they had had the operation. The wiser, more experienced cardiac patient who had redeveloped all of his symptoms three to five years after his first operation knew this was not true. The other depressing aspect of treating cardiac patients is the inevitable loss of the pumping action of the heart with recurrent heart attacks.

Over the past 20 to 30 years there has been a growing trend suggesting healthy lifestyle can affect long term health. If you read the literature carefully, it becomes obvious that a combination of all the lifestyle interventions can be of profound benefit to cardiac patients and patients without established heart disease.

5

CHAPTER ONE

In my practice, I have witnessed two separate types of patients, the motivated and the unmotivated. I can barely remember one truly motivated patient who required repeat coronary artery bypass grafting. On the other hand I can remember numerous unmotivated patients whose grafts blocked within a few years.

Motivation to do what, you may ask? The answer is obvious — it is motivation to change your lifestyle. It can't just be an isolated event such as giving up smoking or not eating as many cakes, biscuits or ice cream. It has to be a global approach, involving how we eat, how we exercise and how we manage our day-to-day stresses.

The responsibility is also on the medical profession to manage the other aspects of health that are out of the patient's hands, such as management of cholesterol levels and related disorders, blood pressure management, treatment of diabetes, and the detection of and counselling for the hereditary components of heart problems. It is up to you to follow the guidelines suggested in this book and make a commitment to yourself.

It was a sobering statistic to find early on in my medical career that 80% of money people spend on their health is in the last five years of their life. It may come as a shock to you to realise the enormous costs to the community, and to you, of having a heart attack, coronary artery bypass operation or a stroke. The cost of comprehensive preventative assessment using high-powered technology and an in-depth risk profile, supervised by a skilled cardiologist, is minuscule in comparison. I believe these assessments and subsequent changes in lifestyle can add ten to 15 effective years to your life. This is opposed to a miserable existence once you have developed serious diseases such as severe heart disease, cancer or chronic lung disease.

One of the problems with the preventative message is that it takes time to sit and discuss all aspects of lifestyle with you. It is often between half an hour to an hour's effort. This may be the most important hour you can spend, as it may influence your behaviour indefinitely. Unfortunately, the medical profession has become somewhat mechanistic. You attend a doctor with, for example, chest pain. He performs a test and says, 'No, this is not cardiac, so it is not my problem.' No explanation is given for the pain, no treatment is suggested, nor any future risk assessed. What is the possibility of that person developing heart disease?

Thirty to 40 years ago there were the pink pills and the green pills and they were usually the same. This was all a doctor could offer in terms of treatment for the patient, but the medical profession's reputation was almost second to none. Why was this? The doctor would sit and listen to the patient! I believe time is the most important commodity we can give our patients. No one listened to James Fixx or the Asian businessman, and they are now both dead. It's too late for them, but with the right advice and the right attitude it may not be too late for you.

This book deals with the individual aspects of lifestyle already mentioned in this chapter. You may need guidance in some areas and find some of the chapters irrelevant to you. If you are a non-smoker (and I hope for your sake you are) then you may wish to jump the chapter on cigarettes, although there is a very interesting section on passive smoking which will justify asking for a smoke-free zone 20 metres around your body.

The second chapter explains heart disease and its treatment in detail. It also explains some of the many questions you may have regarding the biggest killer in our society. Some may find it too technical and wish to skip over parts of this section.

What is this book about? It is trying to show you the way to achieve health by taking a balanced approach to all aspects of your life. Health is not just about avoiding fatty foods and eating more vegetables. It is not just about donning the leotards or running shoes. It is definitely about achieving a balance between five interconnected aspects of your life.

The five point way

1. Physical: How you eat, how you exercise.
2. Mental: Acquisition of knowledge; how stimulating do you find your job?
3. Emotional: Do you value relationships with those close to you? Do you feel happy, how often do you laugh?
4. Sensual: Is your life very mechanical and concrete or do you look for the beauty in life and nature?
5. Spiritual: Do you feel a sense of inner peace? Do you have a belief system that allows you to strive towards higher goals?

It is the combination of all of these factors that leads to health. You will find throughout the book the common theme of five. This is no coincidence. Nature intended five or its multiples to regulate our lives, from our five senses to five digits on one limb.

If you want the answers to the questions posed regarding the five case studies or, more importantly, to the questions you have about maintaining your own health, then read on. I'm sure you'll find it not only informative but also entertaining!

CHAPTER 2

Coronary Heart Disease -
What Is It?

The five components of your heart

Your heart is an organ. Its major function is to pump blood around the body. It is made up of five different components.

The pericardium is the covering around the heart protecting it from external injury and infection, and assisting in the pressure changes within the heart. The valves divide the heart into four separate chambers which open and close. The valves are passive structures which open due to pressure differences within the chambers.

There is an electrical system that sends messages through the heart muscle to tell it to beat. The major bulk of the heart is made up of heart muscle which does the actual pumping work. The fifth component of the heart is made up of coronary arteries, which are hollow tubes carrying blood to the heart muscle to give it the oxygen and other nutrients it needs for normal functioning.

Coronary heart disease is a progressive narrowing of the three major arteries. Varying terms have been used for coronary heart disease over the years including atherosclerosis (hardening of the arteries), myocardial infarction (heart attack), angina pectoris (chest pain) and coronary occlusion (obstruction of an artery). One is reminded of the lady who was told by her cardiologist that she had had a heart attack and her reply was, 'Thank God I didn't have a coronary occlusion.'

A heart attack is caused by a complete blockage in a coronary artery, usually damaging the heart muscle irreparably. Angina pectoris is caused by a partial blockage in an artery so that when a person with a blockage exercises they don't get enough oxygen to the heart muscle and they develop pain in the chest. This pain can also occur at times of high anxiety.

What causes coronary heart disease?

There are numerous risk factors that cause coronary heart disease. Not everyone with these risk factors will develop heart trouble. But if one of these factors is operating in your life you have a much higher chance of developing heart trouble and you or your doctor should be trying to do something about it.

The Five Major Risk Factors
1. Saturated fat intake
2. Cholesterol
3. Cigarettes
4. High blood pressure
5. Family history

The Five Minor Risk Factors
1. Diabetes
2. Obesity

3. Physical inactivity

4. Alcohol

5. Stress

The most important risk factor is probably your cholesterol level. Closely associated with this is the amount of saturated fat you eat. Cigarette smoking is also a major contributing factor, but not all cigarette smokers will develop heart disease and not all people with heart disease will be cigarette smokers.

High blood pressure is an extremely important risk factor for coronary heart disease. Years of high blood pressure can thicken up the walls of the heart and in people over the age of 65 this heart thickness (known as left ventricular hypertrophy), is the most powerful risk factor in the development of coronary heart disease. This can occasionally be detected on a cardiogram but the best test is echocardiography or ultrasound of the heart. Modern cardiac and blood pressure drugs can now reverse this thickening process, especially if detected early.

Genetics is a big risk factor in coronary disease. If you were clever enough to select parents who lived well into their eighties without heart disease, then you have a very good chance of doing the same (especially if you look after yourself). If one of your parents died in their thirties or forties of coronary heart disease it is vital that you have regular, thorough assessments by a cardiologist and also consider specific treatment related to whatever underlying disorder is present.

These five things — saturated fat intake, cholesterol and fat metabolism, cigarette smoking, high blood pressure and family history — are the major risk factors for heart disease. There are a number of minor (though still important) risk factors. These include diabetes (either younger or older onset), obesity, physical inactivity, stress, excessive alcohol consumption and, surprisingly, gout. If you have any of these factors operating in

11

your life, then it is important to discuss them with your doctor to decide whether further evaluation is necessary.

High risk groups

I believe there are three groups of people without any cardiac symptoms whatsoever who should be evaluated on a regular basis.

1. Anyone over the age of 35 with significant risk factors for heart disease, especially males. If you have a family history of premature coronary disease — that is a parent, brother or sister who died in their thirties or forties of this condition — I would suggest an evaluation earlier than 35.

2. People movers should have a check-up. I must say I would not like to be travelling on a plane, a bus or a train if I knew the people driving or flying had not had regular evaluations of their heart to prove their cardiovascular fitness. I believe this should also be extended to taxi drivers. It has been shown with psychological testing that driving taxis is a stressful occupation and if these people have an accident at work it can not only kill them but also their passengers and other people on the road. Being a stressful, sedentary job, I believe there is strong argument for regular testing of taxi drivers.

3. Those people in stressful occupations. Most people have some degree of atherosclerosis and excessive stress is one of the major factors in triggering a heart attack.

Heart attack

People often say to me, 'My next-door neighbour went off to the doctor for a heart check and was told there was nothing wrong with their heart. The next day he had a major heart attack.' This was not the fault of the doctor, the fault of the patient or the fault of the test used but the fault of the disease.

Coronary heart disease is not always a slow, relentless, progressive blockage in an artery. Conditions such as acute heart attacks or unstable angina or sudden cardiac death occur because of different processes.

Basically what happens is that there is a fat build-up in the lining of the arteries with the deposition of cholesterol in the walls. In fact, there can be quite major cholesterol deposition throughout the walls without actually causing any obvious blockages to show up on angiograms. A normal angiogram does not completely exclude the presence of coronary heart disease. It certainly excludes the presence of major blockages but a heart attack can occur rapidly at a site in an artery that appeared as a mild irregularity or a minor blockage on an angiogram the day before.

The reason for this that is the fatty build-up in the area renders the wall weak and thin. Any stress, whether the stress is caused by an argument with another person, smoking one cigarette, performing heavy, physical activity or extreme cold, can lead to the rupturing of this fatty plaque.

It is like standing on the sandbanks of a river and watching it suddenly give way into the water. If you put a fat person in a small pair of trousers and get them to bend over, the trousers will rip. So can the lining of the artery rip over a fatty, weakened area.

When the artery rips internally, or in other words the plaque ruptures, blood rushes into the wall and forms a bruise. A clot forms over the top of the bruise in an attempt to stop the swelling, but both of these processes encroach on the lumen or the inner aspect of the artery, blocking it off. If it blocks off completely, this will lead to a heart attack. If it only partially blocks off, this will lead to unstable angina.

CHAPTER TWO

Lifestyle changes

Understanding the basic mechanisms of heart disease, the causes, and the methods of treating the condition are aspects of the problem. But the most important aspect of treating heart disease is being motivated to introduce the necessary lifestyle changes.

There are not many of us in society who have total balance in our life. Some of us are overweight, some of us eat too much fatty food, some smoke, some drink too much, some don't exercise enough or some of us are under too much stress. Maybe only certain chapters in this book will be relevant to you and give you the right advice to get you back on track. It is important to realise that not one of us is perfect and there are times when we will deviate slightly from the necessary path. This is no great problem, but it is important that most of the time you follow the lifestyle programme suggested.

How can we assess coronary heart disease?

The best method a doctor can follow in assessing risks and possible symptoms of coronary heart disease is to listen to what you are saying. An accurate history of your symptoms gives an excellent indication as to the presence or absence, and severity, of the underlying condition. Chest pain in the centre of the chest radiating down the left arm and associated sweating and shortness of breath, is not always the norm. Symptoms from the nose to the umbilicus can indicate heart disease.

One interesting man with severe heart disease presented stating that when he exercised to any significant level he commenced sneezing. His sceptical doctor performed an exercise test and found that at a certain level of exercise he commenced sneezing. This coincided with marked changes on his cardiogram. Abnormal changes in his coronary angiogram confirmed he had severe heart disease with blockages in three major vessels. When these blockages were bypassed with surgery his sneezing stopped and his exercise test was normal.

This story is not told to worry all those chronic hay fever sufferers, but merely to illustrate the fact that heart disease does not always present in a typical fashion. I have seen numerous patients with a pain in their left elbow or a pain in their teeth, when exerting themselves or at times of rest, who turned out to have significant coronary heart disease. I have also seen patients who have pain in their chest on walking to work in the morning. They could then climb up and down ladders and walk up and down stairs all day without any symptoms, their pain returning during their walk home.

I saw another man in his late forties who presented complaining of chest discomfort only after a meal. He was a very keen tennis player and stated that if he played tennis on an empty stomach he had no symptoms but when he played tennis after a meal he would develop quite severe pain and have to stop his game. Most people would think this man was suffering some digestive problem and reassure him accordingly.

When I performed an exercise test on this man after a Chinese meal it demonstrated quite marked changes, despite the fact that three months previously he had a normal exercise test on an empty stomach. A coronary angiogram was performed because of the significant differences between the two tests. It revealed a 99% obstruction in the major artery in his heart (known as the left main coronary artery).

The man was referred for urgent coronary artery bypass surgery and during the procedure his heart almost stopped. The skill of the surgeon, the late Victor Chang, saved the man's life and he is still very well today. So although the history a person gives is the most important determinate, it is still very important to perform objective testing of the heart.

Everyone with suspected heart disease (or needing a good health screen) should have routine blood tests including estimates of their cholesterol, triglycerides, good cholesterol level (HDL cholesterol), blood sugar level and uric acid, along with a basic full blood count, assessment of kidney function, electrolytes and liver function tests. This comprehensive health screen gives your doctor an excellent indication of your body organs' function and health. For a male, I would also suggest a prostate blood test and for a female, a breast examination, pap smear and possibly an estimation of hormonal levels.

A chest x-ray and cardiogram should be performed. The next step would be an exercise test of some form. Stress testing, such as riding a push bike or walking on a treadmill while under heart monitoring is the best method of assessing for coronary heart disease.

Often a patient will say they develop chest pain with minimal exertion and then are able to perform between 10 to 15 minutes of constant exercise on a treadmill. Other people play down their symptoms, saying they can exercise quite well, yet they can only go for a few minutes on the treadmill and show significant symptoms and marked changes on their cardiogram.

In all patients with coronary heart disease it is important to have some form of exercise testing regardless of whether or not they are having a coronary angiogram. The reason is that although a person's history is the most important part of the evaluation, it is also very important to have an objective evaluation to determine the need for further treatment.

The problem with this particular test is that although it is relatively inexpensive it is not particularly accurate. If you line up 100 people with known heart trouble and perform a basic stress test you will only diagnose coronary disease in 50-60% of cases. You miss at least 40% of people with disease.

If you perform a stress test on 100 people with normal

hearts you will pick up 30 abnormal tests. You would falsely diagnose 30 people with heart disease when they are completely normal. There must be a more accurate method.

To achieve accuracy other methods such as nuclear scanning of the heart and, more recently, the use of ultrasound before, during and after exercise have been widely applied in diagnosing coronary heart disease. Both these investigations markedly increase the diagnostic ability for the evaluation of coronary heart disease, and accurately estimate the severity of the condition. Nuclear testing is more expensive than ultrasound testing and it also requires an injection of nuclear material.

Over the past few years a new test for early screening of heart disease has been developed. Electron Beam Tomography has saved many lives and was developed by a brilliant San Francisco engineer, Doug Boyd. There are 30 centres in North America and 30 in Japan with another 30 around the world.

This test detects calcium in the coronary arteries. Calcium acts as a marker for fat build up and in turn coronary artery disease. Numerous studies have confirmed its almost 100% accuracy. My own feeling is, if you are over 40 and have a heart then you should have an EBT scan because the earlier you are aware of your own risk, the less damage you do to your heart.

The 'gold standard' for the investigation of coronary heart disease is the coronary angiogram. A coronary angiogram involves the puncturing of an artery in the groin or the arm and the insertion of a long wire with a catheter to flush dye through the coronary arteries. During this procedure the dye flushing through the arteries is filmed. This gives an accurate assessment of the presence and severity of blockages in the coronary arteries.

It is essential to have a coronary angiogram before coronary artery surgery or ballooning of the coronary arteries to allow the surgeon to know exactly where he should place the vein or artery grafts and to know exactly how many grafts are necessary. The procedure requires at least an eight to 10 hour stay in hospital and sometimes the patient may be admitted for a day or two. It is very safe but, like any invasive procedure, occasionally it can have complications. The possible complications of coronary angiography include local bleeding at the site of arterial puncture, which can cause quite significant bruising. Occasional dye reactions have been seen and it is important to report any allergies to a cardiologist prior to the test. Patients with severe heart disease have occasionally had heart attacks during the procedure but this complication is, thankfully, extremely rare. Not all people with coronary heart disease or a suggestion of this condition need to have a coronary angiogram. This decision should be made by the cardiologist with full explanation to the patient.

How can coronary heart disease be treated?

There are two basic approaches to the treatment. It may be therapy directed at the consequences of the blockages: drug treatment to relieve angina, coronary balloon angioplasty to open up an obstructed artery, or coronary artery bypass grafting to bypass an obstructed artery with either an arterial or a vein graft.

The neglected aspect of heart disease is the treatment of the factors that caused it in the first place. I have already mentioned in this chapter all the possible risk factors for coronary heart disease. Without careful attention to all of these factors, the disease is a progressive and unrelenting condition.

One can take anti-anginal drugs, have coronary angioplasty or coronary artery surgery but the blockages will not go away with drug treatment nor will the blockages stay away with the more invasive treatment. The only method that has been shown to halt the progression or at times reverse the disease has been a total rearrangement of lifestyle and a new approach to risk factor control.

There are several categories of drugs available for the treatment of angina.

1. The nitrates
2. The beta blockers
3. The calcium channel blockers
4. The anti-platelet agents such as aspirin
5. The anti-coagulants such as heparin, an intravenous preparation, or warfarin, an oral preparation

The treatment of a heart attack is now very complex. Thirty years ago a person with a heart attack was told to rest in bed and keep quiet for a six week period. There were no drugs available and the patient basically had to take their chances.

When someone is admitted to hospital in the 1990s with an acute heart attack, the casualty department becomes like a battle field with different high-powered drugs being infused intravenously in an attempt to melt clots, open arteries and prevent ongoing damage from the heart attack.

The death rate from heart attacks 30 to 40 years ago was around 30% in the six weeks after the attack. These days in most centres this has been reduced to between 3% to 5%. Every month new advances in the treatment of coronary heart disease are being published in medical journals. Each year we are inching towards a negligible mortality from coronary heart disease, but people are still being disabled by this deadly killer.

To have a heart attack in the 1990s costs around $US30,000. One coronary artery bypass procedure costs $US30,000. One stroke costs $US40,000. One cardiac transplant costs $US150,000. Surely there has to be a cheaper alternative?

If a person is not responsive to drug treatment or if the tests show that the severity of the condition is such that medication will probably not have the desired effect, more aggressive treatment is considered.

The two mainstays are ballooning, or stenting, of arteries and coronary artery bypass grafting. Both of these are very successful but again there is a high incidence of recurrence with both procedures. With coronary angioplasty (ballooning) the recurrence rate after the procedure is approximately 30% to 40% within 12 months. With coronary artery surgery after 10 years only 40% of vein grafts are open. Fortunately around 90% to 95% of arterial grafts are still functioning after 10 years which makes this a viable alternative.

If you have coronary heart disease, are on pills, have had a balloon angioplasty to the artery or even coronary artery bypass grafting, it does not mean you are cured of the condition. It is vital in all of these cases to have a 'lifestyle transplant' because this is the most important treatment for coronary heart disease.

I don't believe you can do it all by yourself. If you have heart disease, or want to prevent heart disease, you need to have a close working relationship with your doctor. He or she needs to manage the factors such as cholesterol level and blood pressure, and other problems such as angina and heart failure. Comments made in this book should be seen more as a complement and a supplement to this vital management.

Management of Coronary Heart Disease

1. Diagnosis
2. Risk factor control
3. Medication
4. Angioplasty or stenting
5. Coronary artery bypass grafting

CHAPTER 3

Do We Live to Eat or Eat to Live?

Is there really a link between diet and disease? Is there any truth in the statement that one man's meat is another man's poison? Eating is truly one of life's pleasures (it certainly rates in the top three that I can think of).

Almost weekly there is a new scare regarding different sorts of foods or a new miracle food that will save the world from all its ills. If we believe all we hear, then every type of food can cause cancer. But what really is our current level of knowledge in the 1990s?

High risk of heart disease in world population

Genetic factors

If you look at Asian society, the rate of heart disease is rapidly increasing. Around 50% of people will die from some form of vascular (blood vessel) disease. Another 30% will die from cancer. There is a direct link between vascular disease and saturated fat intake. There is also a link (though not as strong) between saturated fat intake and breast and bowel cancer.

The other 40% of deaths don't appear to be related to dietary intake. The big challenge is therefore to find which individuals in any particular population will be affected by the food they eat. Life is a balance between our genetics and our environment.

There are a few individuals in society who are highly intelligent and a few individuals who are below average intelligence. Most of us are in the middle. The same can be said for the distribution of height, weight and many other characteristics. This also applies to the influence of genetics and our environment. Some people are gravely affected by their genetics. Others have a healthy genetic disposition.

There are certain people who, no matter whether they follow all the right principles of living, eat the right foods, exercise regularly and do everything possible to reduce their stresses, will still have serious diseases occurring at an early age.

This explains the death of the Asian businessman. The main reason he died at the age of 42 was that his father also died at the age of 42 from exactly the same condition. With intensive management of his genetic and metabolic condition he may have lived longer, but on the other hand his destiny may not have been changed at all.

At the other end of the spectrum are those people who do all the wrong things but have such a strong genetic constitution that they appear immune to all sorts of diseases and die in their late seventies or early eighties. This explains our 76-year-old construction worker. Fortunately, or unfortunately, most of us lie somewhere in the middle. Our genetics will still determine our disease processes but the age we develop these diseases will be determined by our environment.

The people of Finland, Scotland and Eastern Europe have

the highest incidence of coronary heart disease in the world. They also have the highest intake of saturated fat.

Saturated fat is the fat found in red meat and in dairy products, especially the non-fermented products such as butter, milk and cream. Coconuts and coconut oil are also a very high source of saturated fats. Both Fins and Scots enjoy eating fish and herring is their preferred choice. Fish consumption lowers your risk of coronary heart disease. Scotland is the home of Scotch whisky and both Finland and Scotland have a very high spirit intake and drink little wine.

Other Western countries such as Australia and America have always been in the mid to slightly higher range in incidence of coronary heart disease. Australia's incidence of coronary heart disease was at its highest in the 1960s and over the past 30 years the death rate has fallen by around 60%. I believe a major reason for this has been the strong lifestyle message emanating from the medical profession.

The saturated fat message has not been as strong in countries such as the British Isles where there is ongoing consumption of large amounts of saturated fat. Not surprisingly the incidence of coronary heart disease in places like the British Isles (where the preventative message has not filtered through), has not changed over the last 30 years. The British Isles act as a wonderful control group for countries that are changing their eating habits.

So while the people of Finland and Scotland continue to die at a rapid rate from coronary heart disease related to high consumption of saturated fat, what about the other cultures around the world?

Disease and Diet

There is no doubt that there is a direct link between coronary heart disease and dietary intake. In South-East Asia and India coronary heart disease is on the increase. Infectious diseases such as malaria, tuberculosis and other exotic infections were the big killers. As the major cities in the Asian countries become more urbanised, the incidence of coronary heart disease rises. This is not just related to people's eating habits but also their smoking habits.

In China and Japan, where the average fat consumption is around 10% of the energy intake per day, there is a very low incidence of coronary heart disease. If you follow the Japanese or Chinese who have emigrated away from their homelands to areas where there is a higher consumption of saturated fat the incidence of coronary heart disease rises.

A study known as the Honolulu Heart Study followed Japanese moving from Japan to Honolulu and then to mainland North America. There was a gradual increase in the incidence of coronary heart disease from Japan to Honolulu and then a higher incidence from Honolulu to North America. Interestingly, this level never rose to the American level of coronary heart disease.

It is also interesting to note that there was a delay of approximately 20 years after saturated fat was introduced to this population, before the occurrence of coronary heart disease. The conclusions are that the Chinese and Japanese are protected to a great extent against coronary heart disease because of their very low fat diet.

What then of the French? The French population as a whole has a 50% less incidence of coronary heart disease compared with most of its European neighbours. The more urban a population becomes, the higher its incidence of coronary heart disease. Therefore, the incidence of coronary heart disease in central Paris is completely different to the incidence of coronary heart disease in southern France and other rural areas of

France. The southern French have a diet and lifestyle more in line with the Italian population.

This has been studied extensively and one of the big factors is the lifelong consumption of red wine by French people. Unfortunately, the incidence of liver disease is very high in France.

The French do not eat much red meat and enjoy fresh vegetables and fruit. They tend to have a moderate alcohol intake and low saturated fat diet which explains their low incidence of heart trouble.

So let us now travel to the small island of Crete off the south eastern tip of Greece. The men and women of Crete have the lowest incidence of heart disease in the Western world. This is despite the fact that 40% of their energy consumption is fat. Most of this fat consumption is in monounsaturated fat from olive oil.

The low risk coronary Cretan male

He is a shepherd or small farmer, a beekeeper, a fisherman, or a tender of olives or vines. He walks to work daily and labours in the soft light of his Greek isle midst the droning of crickets and the bray of distant donkeys, in the peace of his land ... His midday, main meal is of eggplant, with large livery mushrooms, crisp vegetables and country bread dipped in the nectar that is golden Cretan olive oil. Once a week there is a bit of lamb ... Once a week there is chicken. Twice a week there is fish fresh from the sea ... Other meals are hot dishes of legumes seasoned with meats and condiments ... The main dish is followed by a tangy salad, then by dates, Turkish sweets, nuts or fresh succulent fruits. A sharp local wine completes this varied and savoury cuisine. This living pattern, repeated six days a week, is climaxed by a happy Saturday evening. The ritual family dinner is followed by relaxing fellowship with peers. Festivity builds up to a passionate midnight dance under the brilliant moon in the field circle where the grain of the region is winnowed ... On Sunday he strolls to worship with his children and wife. In church he listens to good sense preached by the orthodox priest, a respected leader involved in turn with his own family and his political and religious responsibilities ... He relishes the natural rhythmic cycles and contrasts of his culture: work and rest, solitude and socialisation, seriousness and laughter, routine and revelry ... His is the lowest heart attack risk, the lowest death rate and the greatest life expectancy in the Western world.

Dr Henry Blackburn *American Journal of Cardiology* Vol. 58, 1 July 1988

The low risk hypertensive and coronary Italian woman

The low coronary risk woman lives in Umbria, Italy ... [she] is a nun in a secluded order. Her daily living pattern alternates worship, prayer and manual work ... she is a skilled seamstress and embroiderer, a clever gardener and tender of olives and vines, a keen chicken farmer and swine breeder. From time to time she is also a teacher. Her activities are performed in the peace of the nunnery, ... She may lack competitive drive but she is physically and mentally alert. At the end of the morning's religious celebration and work, she rests and devotes herself to social contact with her peers. Then she continues the day's work with fervour and efficiency. Her midday main meal is pasta with tomatoes, potatoes, legumes, crisp lettuce dressed with light, tasty Umbrian olive oil, homemade wholemeal bread, sweets, fruits and wine. Twice a week she eats a bit of pork seasoned with natural condiments; once a week there is chicken; on Friday there is fresh fish or local cheese. She enjoys walking in the nunnery garden, softly chatting and socialising with other nuns in the sweet, green Francescan landscape, surrounded by sunny terraces. There is time in every day for a relaxation period of meditation. She respects the natural daily rhythm of wakefulness and sleep, and faces the existential problems with joy. Her blood pressure does not increase with age, hypertension is unknown in the nunnery. Coronary heart disease is absent up to a very old age. She has very low risk for brain or heart attack and one of the lowest early death rates and longest life expectancies of all women in the civilized world.

Mario Timio MD *American Journal of Cardiology* 60:1177, 1987

It is interesting that in our busy stressful lives we dream of having a few weeks off and living exactly as these people live all year round. Maybe it would be boring after a couple of months but wouldn't we like to try it?

It appears from these two people's lives that there is some protective element in olive oil which prevents the development of coronary heart disease. There is no doubt that the people of Crete and other Mediterranean countries do have a low incidence of coronary heart disease and a significant longevity compared with other Westerners. Although I am not foolish enough to believe that diet is the only factor, I feel it has a major influence on the development of coronary heart disease.

What about the Eskimos? It is said that coronary heart disease in this population is almost non-existent. The possibility is that the very high intake of fish prevents coronary heart disease. There is no doubt that fish is protective against heart disease. Numerous scientific studies have been conducted on this topic. A large population study from Norway published in the *New England Journal of Medicine* in the 1980s showed that having at least two fish meals per week reduced the risk of developing heart disease. This has been supported by many other studies.

What is it in fish that is so protective? For many years it was felt to be the high proportion of polyunsaturated fats, especially an omega-3 fatty acid known as eicosapentaenoic acid. This chemical binds to the platelets, which are sticky little cells running around the blood stream forming clots with another chemical known as fibrin.

Aspirin works to thin the blood by preventing the action of platelets forming clots. If you have recently taken aspirin and then shaved your face or legs and cut yourself, you bleed much more easily. This is aspirin's effect on platelets.

Eicosapentaenoic acid is the natural anti-platelet (anti-clotting) substance found in fish. It is felt that a high proportion of fish meals can thin out the blood and in some cases prevent coronary heart disease. This is the best explanation for the Eskimos' very low incidence of heart disease.

You may say I'll start eating more fish. The big problem with this is that we must all die of something and the Eskimos do not live any longer than we do. Blood vessels change in one of two ways when we get into our sixties, seventies, eighties and nineties. The fact is that no matter how healthy you are, once you reach old age, your blood vessels lose some of their tone in the way everyone's skin will develop some wrinkles as we age. If you consume a high saturated fat diet these blood vessels with reduced tone will also become clogged with fat. If you live in a population where there is a low saturated fat, high fish diet, such as the Eskimos', the blood vessels still lose their tone and instead of becoming clogged with fat become friable and weakened, leading to rupture of the walls. Eskimos die at the same age as we do of cerebral haemorrhage rather than coronary heart disease. They rupture blood vessels in the brain and bleed internally. One could argue that they would prefer to die of a short sharp heart attack than a cerebral haemorrhage.

Fat and weight

Why do we eat at all? It is not just to calm our hunger. We need food for energy. Without a certain level of kilojoules every day we would die from starvation. This basically means that the cells are starved of vital nutrients which keep them working. These vital nutrients include glucose, fatty acids, cholesterol and protein. Vitamins and minerals are also essential in this equation. The average Asian diet is around 15% to 20% fat, 20% to 25% protein and the rest some form of carbohydrate, often sugar, but also complex carbohydrates. The average Western diet is 30 to 35 % fat, 20 to 25% protein and the remainder carbohydrates.

Let me discuss eating habits. It is a very simple equation, energy gained versus energy expended. What goes in must be used as energy and, if it isn't, you'll put on weight. It is safe to say that for a person over the age of 35, an average safe kilojoule intake lies somewhere between 5000 to 7000 kilojoules per day depending on the activity of that person. Food gives energy, and activity burns it off. Without any exercise we require around 3360 kilojoules. To perform heavy exercise every day probably burns off around 16,800 kilojoules. For example, people going on Antarctic treks would expend around 21,000 to 25,000 kilojoules per day and therefore have to take in that amount of food to maintain their weight.

The best source of kilojoules for energy is saturated fat but it is also the best source of extra weight. It is certainly not an efficient source of energy for that reason. For example, a fit 18-year-old sportsman may burn off 16,800 kilojoules per day in energy but may also take in 16,800 kilojoules a day to maintain his weight.

Once we get into ages above 35, when our high powered activity decreases, we may only need half that amount. Even a slight increase might put on weight. As we get older our metabolism slows down and it is easier to gain and harder to lose weight. The younger you are when you try to lose weight, the easier it will be. This does not mean that if you are in your fifties, sixties or seventies and are overweight you should not try, but you must set yourself realistic goals.

Unfortunately the body is not like a car. When you put fuel in a car it will sit in the tank until you drive the car. If you put fuel in the body and don't use that fuel, it will be stored in the body as fat. The more fat that is stored, the harder it is to shift. This is one of the depressing aspects of dieting. The first month or so, you may be encouraged by the loss of a few kilograms but you are shifting the most recent fat stores only. They are easy to shift. Over the next six months or so the fat is much harder to move, and despite your best efforts it may be very slow in coming off.

If you are serious about losing weight, it is important to have a sensible eating plan and couple this with a sensible exercise plan. As I will reinforce in later chapters, if you are not a regular exerciser do not immediately rush out and perform exercise, unless you have had a thorough health screen by a doctor. This is one of the common causes of people dropping dead in the street. They think, 'I'm unfit', and immediately start exercising, going out for a jog. A recent article in the *New England Journal of Medicine* showed that non-exercisers who perform some extreme form of heavy exercise are 100 times more likely to have an acute heart attack than people who exercise regularly.

If you are going to exercise get assessed by your doctor and then gradually ease into it. I suggest that to lose weight you should have a hearty breakfast, a moderate lunch and a small evening meal. The ideal way to eat is to have a good breakfast, lunch as the main meal, a sleep after lunch, work in the afternoon and a very light evening meal, followed by some exercise.

There was one elegant and extremely simple study in which an amount of food was given over a week to three different

groups of people. Group one ate all this food in the one sitting per day for seven days. Group two had the same amount of food spaced over three meals for seven days, and the third group had the same amount in six smaller meals each day, for seven days.

The results were astounding. Group one put on weight, group two stayed the same and group three lost weight despite having exactly the same quantity of food throughout the day. My explanation for this is that smaller amounts of fuel were injected into the system every day, allowing the group that ingested the food six times a day to have much smaller saturated fat and sugar loads. This allowed for a more efficient metabolism which increased the basal metabolic rate and used the limited amounts of fuel available at the time.

At the other end of the spectrum, the group that had only one meal a day but ingested the same amount of food, put a high fat and glucose load on the metabolising tissues, leading to a lower basal metabolic rate. Starvation for the rest of the day lowered basal metabolic rate. The excess fuel that was injected into the system once was laid down in fat stores. This work was backed up in another study from the *New England Journal Of Medicine*, which showed that 17 snack meals every day during the waking hours led to weight loss, compared with stable weight when a person had the same amount of food over three meals.

You may be one of those very busy people who feels breakfast and lunch are unimportant meals and have no time to eat. By the time you arrive home you are absolutely starving having had minimal food during the day, apart from the occasional cup of coffee and possibly a biscuit or cake to keep your energy levels up. Despite the fact that you don't eat breakfast or lunch, you wonder why you continue to gain weight, or not lose any weight. I hope the answer is now obvious.

There are many claims regarding wonderful diets that can help you lose five to six kilograms in a month. This may be achieved, but it is not through the loss of fat, it is the loss of water and muscle. An average 65 kilogram man has about 38 litres of water distributed throughout the body, in the cells and other tissues. Most fad diets are designed to deplete the body of this water and some muscle goes with it, but the real of aim of any diet should be to lose fat. This is a very slow process that can take months. So when you decide to change your eating habits, don't expect to see a marked weight loss in the first 3 months. Aim over 6 to 12 months to lose a significant amount of weight. In 19 to 20 meals of 21 meals a week we should be very rigid with what we eat. The other one or two meals can include the occasional piece of dessert or fatty treat that you crave and enjoy.

Evolution to the Population Explosion

Through the ages people, in their desire to avoid the inevitable, have been on the quest for immortality. Commencing with the

WEIGHT FOR HEIGHT CHART
WOMEN

Height Range (without shoes)		AGE IN YEARS				
		18	19-20	21-22	23-24	25+
Ft In	Cm		WEIGHT IN KILOGRAMS			
4 6	137-139	45-38	46-38	47-39	47-39	48-40
4 7	140-141	46-38	46-39	47-39	48-40	49-41
4 8	142-144	46-39	47-40	48-40	48-41	49-42
4 9	145-146	46-41	47-41	48-41	49-42	50-43
4 10	147-149	48-41	48-42	50-42	51-43	51-44
4 11	150-151	50-42	51-43	51-43	52-44	53-45
5 0	152-154	51-44	51-44	52-45	53-46	54-46
5 1	155-156	53-46	53-46	54-46	55-47	56-48
5 2	157-159	54-47	55-48	56-48	57-49	57-49
5 3	160-162	57-48	57-49	58-49	59-50	59-51
5 4	163-164	59-50	60-50	60-51	61-51	61-52
5 5	165-167	61-51	61-51	62-52	63-53	63-54
5 6	168-169	63-52	63-53	64-54	65-55	65-56
5 7	170-172	64-55	65-56	66-56	66-56	67-57
5 8	173-174	66-56	66-56	67-57	68-58	69-59
5 9	175-177	67-59	68-60	69-60	70-61	71-61
5 10	178-179	69-61	70-61	71-62	72-62	72-63
5 11	180-182	71-63	72-63	73-64	74-64	74-65
6 0	183-184	73-65	74-65	75-66	76-66	76-66
6 1	185-187	75-66	76-67	76-67	77-68	78-68
6 2	188	76-68	77-69	78-69	79-70	80-70

MEN

Height Range (without shoes)		AGE IN YEARS				
		18	19-20	21-22	23-24	25+
Ft In	Cm		WEIGHT IN KILOGRAMS			
4 6	137-139	45-38	46-38	47-39	47-39	48-40
5 0	152-154	56-50	61-50	61-51	62-52	63-52
5 1	155-156	57-51	62-51	63-52	64-53	64-54
5 2	157-159	59-52	63-53	64-54	65-55	66-55
5 3	160-162	61-54	65-54	66-55	67-56	67-56
5 4	163-164	66-55	67-56	68-56	69-57	69-58
5 5	165-167	68-56	69-57	70-58	71-59	71-59
5 6	168-169	70-58	71-59	72-60	73-61	73-61
5 7	170-172	72-60	73-61	74-61	75-62	76-63
5 8	173-174	74-61	75-62	76-63	77-64	77-65
5 9	175-177	75-64	77-64	78-65	79-66	79-66
5 10	178-179	77-65	79-66	80-66	81-67	81-68
5 11	180-182	81-67	81-67	82-68	83-69	84-70
6 0	183-184	82-69	84-69	85-70	86-71	86-72
6 1	185-187	85-71	86-71	86-72	88-73	88-74
6 2	188-190	87-72	88-73	89-74	90-75	91-76
6 3	191-192	90-75	91-76	91-76	92-77	93-78
6 4	193	92-77	93-78	94-79	95-80	95-81

Pharaohs, with their elaborate burial chambers and rituals, we move on to the promise of eternal life, a belief in reincarnation and down through the ages from the Holy Grail to modern medicine's attempts to slow the aging process.

The human body is designed to last 50 to 60 years. When the human first evolved from the apes, it was enough of an achievement to survive the ravages of the day. At that stage, ancient humans were just more intelligent members of the food chain and usually met their demise by accident or through the jaws of some hungry animal.

As ancient humans became more organized, they had to deal with not only the ravages of the animal kingdom and mother nature but a new enemy — fellow humans. Conflicts one against one, tribe against tribe, nation against nation have certainly been an excellent form of crowd control.

Since World War Two there have been no great wars to cull population growth and our world population has risen to around six billion. There has been an astronomical growth in science and technology which has gone hand in hand with improvements in sanitation and modern medicine. Our average life spans have risen dramatically. But can this be improved?

Is it possible for us to live a good quality of life well into our eighties and nineties or longer? Can modern medicine and science do this for us? Another moral and philosophical issue is: should modern medicine and science do this for us? Should we be attempting to prolong life in a world where our resources are already being stretched to cater for the present population?

In a world where infant mortality rates are dropping and death rates in the elderly are also dropping there are less slices of cake to go around. I know the answer is very simple. We should be controlling our resources and our population and people shouldn't be living as long because this is a drain on these precious resources.

The problem is when you hear the wings of the angel of

death flapping around your ears you are very happy for those resources to be stretched.

Around ten to 20 years ago there emerged evidence that certain individuals lived 20 to 30 years longer than the rest of us, with a much better quality of life. I can recall watching television documentaries 15 years ago and seeing live footage of people who were allegedly 100 to 110 years old, singing, dancing, riding horses and looking for all the world like they were in their late fifties. I hate to admit it but these people had cigarettes in their mouths. These were the people of the Hunza Valley in Pakistan and certain tribes from Georgia which was then part of the Soviet Union.

Just as people will stream to Lourdes in France for the possibility of cures for terminal illness, people were then streaming to the Hunza Valley and to Georgia to study the lifestyles of these regions. Books were written, documentaries were made, the fountain of youth had been discovered, yes folks, it was all in lifestyle.

The simple stress-free environment, combined with specific Hunza Valley or Georgian diet and climate, was all that one needed to survive well into their late nineties and early hundreds and even have the occasional cigarette.

It took a more cynical researcher from the Massachusetts Institute of Technology who decided that a few weeks in any place could not give the true picture. This fellow decided to do a Ph. D. on why the people of these regions lived for so long. After he was there for six months, the answer was very clear. I am about to give you the secret for the fountain of youth.

Living in the Hunza Valley in Pakistan, or Georgia, is a very peaceful, tranquil existence. Each day the inhabitants of these regions wake to a simple breakfast of nuts, berries and fresh water from a local stream. They toil in the fields all day gathering food for their lunch and evening meals. At night they may sit around a communal fire singing and dancing. This occurs day in and day out and let's face it, it sounds pretty boring!

So the people of these regions have found an excellent way to overcome the boredom, and that is to have birthday parties. Each person would have between five to six birthdays per year throughout their adult life. So someone who says he is 110 years old, but looks 50, is in reality 50! It's a great way to achieve immortality without really trying.

High rates of heart disease

1. Finland
2. Scotland
3. Northern Ireland
4. Eastern Europe
5. Russia and other Soviet states

Low rates of heart disease

1. China
2. Japan
3. France
4. Eskimos
5. Crete and other parts of southern Europe

Increasing rates of heart disease

1. India
2. Malaysia
3. Thailand
4. Indonesia
5. South Pacific

CHAPTER 4

The Good, The Bad
and The Ugly

Saturated fat in meat

The real poison in food is saturated fat. There are several
sources of saturated fat. The first is all forms of meat, especially red meat. The prime cuts of red meat have more fat than the
lean red meat but there is still a significant amount of saturated
fat in any sort of meat. Red meat has the highest proportions,
with less in pork and the game birds. Fried lard and pork fat
are pure sources of saturated fat and there is lot of fat in
sausages. The more fat you eat the more clogged your arteries
become.

Saturated fat in dairy products

Another major source of saturated fat is dairy products. This is
especially true of the unfermented dairy products such as butter, cream and full cream milk. If you are going to use milk,

the low fat milks which are now available everywhere have a very pleasant taste.

What about the fermented dairy products, such as cheese and low fat yoghurt? Firstly, there has never been any study linking the eating of cheese with coronary heart disease. One must look at the Mediterranean nations and the French who eat a significant amount of cheese but have a very low incidence of heart disease. I am not sure what the science behind it is but there appears to be something protective in the fermentation process.

The low fat yoghurts, especially those with acidophilus (a particular type of bacterial culture known as a probiotic) are positively good for you. They assist the normal bacteria living in your gastro-intestinal tract, preventing the nasty viruses and potent bacteria from entering the bloodstream and causing significant infections. Acidophilus yoghurts also assist the breakdown of cholesterol and other fats in the gut, helping to keep the cholesterol lower.

The real killers in Asian cooking are ghee, which is clarified butter or pure butter fat, and coconut products. Butter is pure saturated fat which means ghee and butter should be eliminated from the diet of people with heart disease.

Eggs

The white of the egg contains dietary protein and no significant amounts of fat. It is the yolk that contains all the saturated fat and cholesterol. The recommendation is to eat two to three eggs per week.

Interestingly there was one man in his eighties reported in the *New England Journal of Medicine* who ate around 12 eggs per day who had a normal cholesterol/triglycerides level. There are always exceptions to the rule.

Simple sugars

The hidden source of saturated fat is sugar in foods such as rich desserts, confectionary, biscuits, cakes, ice cream, salty snacks and soft drinks. For those of you who know there is absolutely no fat whatsoever in confectionary, just solid sugar, remember if this sugar is not burned off immediately, it will be converted into fat. So will sweet carbonated drinks and commercial fruit juices.

Most people will criticise you for having two spoonfuls of sugar in your tea or coffee but are quite happy to drink a can of cola which has about six spoonfuls of sugar in it. There is certainly more than 2 spoonfuls of sugar in a 250 millilitre fruit juice. Their comments are obviously expressed through ignorance not hypocrisy.

It is social behaviour when visiting someone for morning or afternoon tea to serve a few biscuits or a piece of cake. It is seen as impolite to refuse the invitation but I believe it is better to decline the offer. I don't know how many times patients have said to me, 'But doctor, I only eat three small meals per day.' When I go into their story I find they have a regular quantity of biscuits, confectionary and cake.

What about ice cream and other desserts? I would like to stress nobody needs to have dessert every night of the week. As I have said before I believe strongly that 19 meals out of 21 per week should be rigid and the other two you can do what you like. Always watch out for the number of desserts you have because these are a rich source of saturated fat and sugar.

Take-away food

One of the scourges of our modern society is take-away food. With more women in the workforce, no one feels like coming home and cooking a full meal. The answer is to either eat out or, more commonly, buy take-away food. It doesn't hurt to have the occasional take-away but I would strongly suggest that you limit the amount and be somewhat discerning about the type of take-away that you buy.

Let's look at what's available. The American style of take-away, such as hamburgers, fried fish and chips, commercial pizzas, the humble meat pie and deep fried chicken with all the herbs and spices will not protect your coronary arteries.

The hamburger, despite the lashings of wonderful fresh salad and a wholesome sesame seed bun, is full of saturated fat. A person on a low fat diet should have 20 grams of saturated fat per day and a person on a more liberal, sensible diet can have 40 grams. If I tell you that an average hamburger contains approximately 10 to 12 grams of saturated fat, you can see that

a meal of a hamburger, French fries and a thickshake would be over the 20 gram mark. The commercial pizza probably has the highest concentration of saturated fat in any of the take-away foods. It's a wonderful thought, isn't it — pan fried coronary arteries!

Deep-fried foods are commonly eaten throughout the world. In Western countries deep-fried fish and potato chips are a popular take-away but are full of saturated fat. Deep-frying is best done in monounsaturated oils rather than the saturated fatty oils (such as lard, dripping or ghee). Even better, avoid deep-fried food altogether as the oil oxidises in the heating process and loses most of its goodness. Also the amount of fat you are eating in deep-fried food is greater than in other cooked food.

What about the Asian take-aways? Chinese food can be quite good for you but if soon after ingesting Chinese food you feel a horrible lump in your stomach and don't feel particularly well, it is likely that the food has been cooked in saturated fat and sprinkled with monosodium glutamate. Monosodium glutamate can cause nausea and arrhythmia (irregular heartbeat). A lot of people are allergic to it and it has been known to cause cancer experimentally.

The Thai and Malaysian take-aways with a peanut oil base (a good monounsaturated fat) are nutritious. On the other hand, coconut oil, which is often used as a base for Thai and Indian soups and curries, is a rich source of saturated fat and should be avoided.

I would suggest that you get into the habit of reading the labels on canned and other processed foods to develop a firm knowledge of the fat, carbohydrate and protein content. Regardless of what sort of fat you are ingesting, there are 39 kilojoules to every gram of fat. This compares to only 17 kilojoules per gram of a protein or carbohydrate.

Monounsaturated oils

What about the food that is good for you? Why do the people of Crete live for around ten years longer than the rest of us, with little heart disease or cancer? The answer is simple. It is partially their lifestyle and partially their genetics. Much of their lifestyle revolves around their eating habits, and despite the fact that 40% of their diet is fat there is little saturated fat and a great proportion of monounsaturated fat, usually in the form of olive oil. It is my suggestion that it is of more benefit to cook in olive oil, especially extra virgin olive oil, than it is to grill your food. I am not suggesting that olive oil will render you immune to saturated fat but I am suggesting that extra virgin olive oil is extremely beneficial to one's health.

With extra virgin olive oil you get better value for money. The first factor is the monounsaturated fats in olive oil lower LDL cholesterol. These fats increase the HDL cholesterol and extra virgin olive oil (as opposed to normal olive oil or the other monounsaturated oils, such as canola) is loaded with antioxidants known as polyphenols.

For cholesterol to get into arteries and clog them, it has to be oxidized first. The more antioxidants in your diet, the less this process can occur. Because extra virgin olive oil is the oil that comes from the first pressing of the olives, it is the most natural and least chemically affected, thus retaining all the natural antioxidants.

The people of Crete cook in extra virgin olive oil and add it to their salads with a bit of balsalmic vinegar. These people do not use butter or margarine but dip their bread in olive oil. So I would see olive oil as a treatment to protect you from heart disease. It also enhances the flavour of food in the process of cooking.

The only acceptable alternatives to olive oil are peanut and canola oil. They contain approximately the same amount of

monounsaturated fats as olive oil but without the antioxidants. The advantage of canola oil is that it contains 10% omega-3 fatty acids. The omega-3 fatty acids are a major component in fish oils. Recent work has suggested a significant reduction in sudden death rates occurs in patients with heart disease who consume canola-based oils in their diet.

Avocado

Another rich source of monounsaturated fats is the much maligned avocado. It has been said for many years that you should avoid avocado and cooking with too much oil because they put on weight. Of course you will put on weight if you have too much, but monounsaturated fat is desirable in the diet.

A good friend of mine, Professor David Colquhoun, did a study using avocados. He added avocado to the normal diet of a group of people for a week, measuring their cholesterol/triglycerides levels at the start and at the end of the programme. He found a significant drop in LDL cholesterol, an elevation in the HDL cholesterol and a reduction in triglycerides. I believe that avocado should be a part of most salads. It can be used as a spread rather than butter or margarine.

Margarine

There has been a great deal of controversy regarding polyunsaturated margarines and polyunsaturated oils. Research shows that polyunsaturated oils, although reducing the bad cholesterol can also have an effect on reducing the good cholesterol levels as well. I feel it is better to lean towards the monounsaturated oils for all situations.

L-arginine

Like all food stuffs L-arginine has been an important part of our dietary intake for many years but only in recent years have we discovered the benefits of this wonderful substance. L-arginine is an essential amino acid. An amino acid is one of the breakdown products of protein. A protein is basically a whole lot of amino acids strung together with a few bits of nitrogen, carbon and hydrogen on the other end.

Some amino acids are manufactured within the body but some are only available in the diet. For example, there is a high proportion of lysine (another amino acid) in saturated fat based foods, especially the red meats, with little L-arginine.

Basically, the more L-arginine you have in your diet the healthier you are. Why is L-arginine so important? One of the major reasons is that when L-arginine enters the body it is converted to a substance known as nitric oxide. I know you're thinking that's the stuff dentists give you to make you laugh. That's nitrous oxide. Nitric oxide, as the more aware among you will realise, was Molecule of the Year in 1992.

In the same way they have Miss World and Miss Universe, they have Molecule of the Year. Not only does the molecule get to travel extensively, meet people, receive honorary doctorates at different universities, and basically have a damn good year, but also gets to be on the cover of the December *Science* magazine. The reason nitric oxide achieved this recognition was its ability to open up blood vessels. You may remember the rupturing of plaques in acute coronary disease. Nitric oxide protects the body against this process. The more L-arginine you have in the diet the more nitric oxide you make and the less coronary disease you have. This is not scientific conjecture but has been shown in studies.

Where do we get L-arginine? We get it in nuts. For many years there has been ongoing criticism of nuts. Are they full of fat? Do they block coronary arteries? A study was done on pigs that were fed peanuts. They developed hardening of the arteries. What the study failed to mention was that the pigs were also given a very high fat diet in addition to the peanuts, and I believe the peanuts were just an innocent bystander.

Nuts are nature's health food. I am not suggesting that if you eat nuts in addition to saturated fat you will be protected. I am suggesting that you should have nuts as a replacement for other foods. Instead of that biscuit or piece of cake for morning tea, have a handful of raw mixed nuts. Nuts are loaded with L-arginine, especially almonds and walnuts. Even the humble peanut is full of L-arginine, monounsaturated fats and, as an extra bonus, a substance known as resveratrol. Resveratrol has numerous benefits, including decreasing blood clotting and dilating blood vessels.

There have been two major studies which show the advantages of eating of nuts. Seventh Day Adventists are a very healthy group of people and numerous studies have shown that they live, on average, around seven years longer than the rest of us. One landmark study, known as The Adventist Health Study, followed the living habits and mortality rates in Seventh

Day Adventists in California over a 30 year period. It demonstrated that in this extremely healthy population, the Seventh Day Adventists who had five nut-based meals per week had 50% less heart disease than their colleagues who did not have the nuts. As you may know, the Seventh Day Adventists often use nut meat as a replacement for normal meat, and use it as a base for much of their food.This study was supported by the

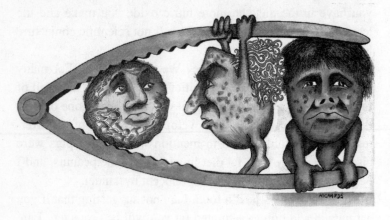

Iowa Women's Study which also showed the same basic result, that five nut-based meals per week reduced the incidence of coronary heart disease by 50%.

So for those of us who aren't vegetarian and don't eat a lot of nut meat, how do we have our five nut-based meals per week? My solution in simple and certainly delicious. I like to start each day with an L-arginine hit. I have three to four dessertspoons of mixed nuts in a bowl, preferably walnuts and almonds, sprinkle some oat bran flake over the top of this (oat-bran has an effect on reducing cholesterol), slice a banana over the top of this, and add low fat flavoured acidophilus yoghurt and low fat milk.This is a delicious way to start the day with a good combination of L-arginine, monounsaturated fats and good healthy complex carbohydrates with fibre.

If you think nuts are fatty it gets back to how much you eat and what foods are being replaced by the nuts.

You'll find L-arginine in plenty in the legumes. Beans, especially fresh beans, are loaded with this wonderful substance. All lentils, alfalfa, snow peas, garlic and onion have a high proportion of L-arginine. Garlic has some other wonderful properties I will discuss later.

Fish

Research on fish suggests that two to three fish meals per week help prevent coronary heart disease. Much of the argument is centred around the polyunsaturated fats (the omega-3 fatty acids) being beneficial components of fish. Work on fish oil capsules has been less rewarding. There have been no studies that have shown a great benefit from fish oil capsules, apart from a couple of studies that have suggested some reduction in re-blockages after balloon angioplasty.

It is interesting that it takes six fish oil capsules per day to have an effect on the platelets, those sticky little substances that block up arteries, and it takes 18 fish oil capsules per day to have an effect in lowering the cholesterol and triglyceride levels. If you take this amount of fish oil capsules you will definitely go around smelling like a fish. I believe the L-arginine content of fish is as beneficial as the omega-3 fatty acid component. You can take L-arginine in tablet form, usually around 10 grams per day, a hefty dose. Why not enjoy it more in your food?

Garlic

Garlic is not only a natural antibiotic substance, it also has quite profound effects on the cardiovascular system, reducing blood coagulation and making the blood thinner and less likely to clot. It has a very strong effect on opening up arteries in the same way that L-arginine does. Part of this is from the L-arginine content. You may not be particularly popular in the workplace or at home, but you'll keep yourself very healthy by ingesting a good amount of fresh garlic.

Mushrooms

Mushrooms are a fungus. They are an excellent source of protein and fibre without any fat. They are a rich source of iron and folic acid, niacin and riboflavin, which are in the vitamin B group, and other essential minerals. There are many types of mushrooms, each with their own health benefits. Researchers suggest the asian Shitake and Reishi mushrooms have anti-cancer properties as well as excellent nutritional value. Mushrooms add complexity and help balance your diet.

Changing your diet

Now that we have rid ourselves of the obsession to have meat as the main staple, what am I suggesting as a substitute? Let's go to the places where they have little coronary disease and see what they eat. Mediterraneans and the asians eat a lot of complex carbohydrates. I am suggesting that either pasta or rice be the bulk of your meals and if you wish to eat meat, use it for flavour, cooked in extra virgin olive oil or peanut oil.

I would suggest five evening meals out of seven per week be based around pasta and rice. The major substance in pasta and rice is complex carbohydrate. Complex carbohydrates provide a steady source of energy without generating hardening of the arteries, heart attacks and strokes. Another rich source of complex carbohydrates is the potato. You can even bake the potato in extra virgin olive oil. Cereals and grainy breads are also very good for you. One study performed in France showed that the two factors that contributed to the much lower incidence of heart disease in the French, compared with other Europeans, were their ingestion of red wine and whole grain breads.

Antioxidants

Fruit and vegetables are a major source of antioxidants in our diet. You basically can't get enough fruit and vegetables. You can replace any food in your diet with fruit and vegetables and you can't go wrong. My suggestion would be for you to have two to three pieces of fruit per day and at least three to four different vegetables per day. There are 600 naturally occurring antioxidants in fruit and vegetables and I don't intend to list them here.

There are different compounds in different types of vegetables and I have already mentioned L-arginine and the natural antibiotics in garlic. We are learning more each day about the important healing properties of fruit and vegetables.

Conclusion

Although we can become very clinical about food, I think it is important to realise that food is one of life's pleasures. A lot that has been said and written about food is either inappropriate or overstated.

If you believed all the scientific work published regarding food you would think that almost every food has the possibility of causing cancer. If you were to isolate certain chemicals in food and take them in toxic doses, you might develop cancer. This means very little because when you eat the food in which the chemical is found there are many other substances that either neutralise the chemical or change its effect, thereby either rendering the substance harmless or making it beneficial to your health.

With food some simple principles are important. Fresh is best. Variety is important and don't eat on the run. Sit down and enjoy your meals. Talk with your friends and family while you are eating and don't miss out on breakfast.

The Right Eating Plan

1. Reduce saturated fats, for example meat, dairy products, junk food and take-away.
2. Increase monounsaturated fats, for example extra virgin olive oil, avocados, nuts.
3. Increase foods containing L-arginine, for example nuts, legumes, onions, garlic and fish.
4. Increase complex carbohydrates, for example pasta, rice, potatoes, cereals and grainy breads.
5. Increase antioxidants, for example red wine, fresh fruit and vegetables, tea, vitamin E

How Sweet It Is —
Diabetes

If I asked you what the cause of diabetes is you would probably say, 'It's too much sugar or not enough insulin.' If I asked you how diabetes should be treated you would probably say, 'If it is only mild, reduce your sugar intake and if it is severe you need insulin injections.' The most simple answers are often wrong and this is certainly the case with these notions of handling diabetes.

Diabetes, and its more subtle manifestations, is extremely common. In a Caucasian population it usually occurs at a rate of around 5% in people over the age of 40. In certain populations scattered throughout the world the rate can be higher than 50%.

What is diabetes?

There are basically two types of diabetes, the first being insulin dependent diabetes and the second, non-insulin dependent diabetes. Insulin dependent diabetes is a less common condition usually occuring in childhood but it can, in fact, occur at any age. It often happens after another illness such as a virus or bacterial infection. The child does not recover, becomes very thirsty and loses a significant amount of weight.

In almost all cases the person afflicted will have to be on insulin for the rest of their lives, having injections between two to four times a day and constantly pricking their fingers to measure blood sugar levels. Without this rather laborious and, at times, frustrating procedure the person cannot achieve good control of their diabetes and has a much greater probability of experiencing complications.

The basic problem in insulin dependent diabetes is that an immune process attacks the pancreas. This is the organ in the abdomen that makes insulin and other unrelated chemicals necessary for digestion. This immune attack profoundly affects the function of the specific cells that make insulin. The resulting absolute lack of insulin requires an injection of a synthetic insulin.

Those affected in childhood can still lead relatively normal lives and there are many great achievers in our society who are diabetic and run large businesses, are champion sports people, have children and manage the day to day rigours of parenthood. Diabetes, therefore, is not a death sentence, only a condition that, with the right motivation and education, can be well-managed.

Non-insulin dependent diabetes is more common but people affected by this form of diabetes tend to be older. These people usually do not need insulin but at times it may be necessary, sometimes in extremely high doses. This is a common condition caused not by obesity or having too much sugar but is, in fact, purely genetic — you either inherit it from your mother or father or from a combination of their genes. The basic defect can be explained by understanding how cells work.

Cells are basically lined up alongside each other in the same way as a line of shops. The road in this case is the blood vessels which carry the nutrients to be delivered to the cell. These nutrients are not just sugar but also include cholesterol, triglycerides and amino acids. These substances are the building blocks for metabolism within the cell — they feed the cell and allow it to work properly. Without these substances the cells malfunction and we all know what happens when this occurs.

Each shopfront along a road has a doorway which must be opened. A cell is very similar. Insulin acts like a doorman opening the door to allow these nutrients to get inside the cel, and the basic problem in non-insulin dependent diabetes and its related syndromes is a resistance to the effects of insulin. If the door doesn't open properly, it makes it very difficult for all of these nutrients to get inside the cell.

You can probably clearly see now that this form of diabetes is not a problem with just sugar but with overall metabolism, leading to the sugar being stuck within the blood vessel system along with cholesterol, triglycerides and other chemicals. This leads to all of these chemicals building up in the lining of large and small blood vessels, and eventually causing blockages.

Insulin resistance is being much more widely recognised as the central factor not only in non-insulin dependent diabetes but also three other very common problems:

1. Hypertension or high blood pressure.

2. Hyperlipidaemia or cholesterol and triglyceride elevation

3. Obesity.

I am not suggesting that all of these people are obese because they possess the insulin resistance syndrome but this does play a part in a significant amount of obesity. It certainly does not give overweight people the excuse to say, 'Oh, it's all in my genes, there is nothing I can do about it.' It actually means that people with the gene for insulin resistance need to work a hell of a lot harder with diet and exercise to keep their weight down.

Everyone with non-insulin dependent diabetes has the gene for insulin resistance. It has been estimated that 50% to 60% of people with high blood pressure also possess this gene and possibly as many as 40% of people with cholesterol abnormalities.

These four factors (non-insulin dependent diabetes, high blood pressure, cholesterol abnormalities, tendency to obesity) either alone or in combination contribute to the fifth factor which is a tendency to atherosclerosis, the major killer in Western society. This is also the emerging killer throughout Asia and India now that saturated fat intake has increased, cigarette smoking is commonplace and stress and pollution are part of urban life.

You may ask, 'Why, when the body has been supposedly designed for balance, is this gene so common in so many people and a major cause of disease and other health problems?'

Although there is no definite answer there are certainly some extremely plausible theories. Many years ago, before the days of television and fast food outlets, our ancestors were mainly hunter-gatherers. Tribes of people would travel from one area to another gathering edible vegetation basically to sustain life. When all the food from one area had been consumed, these tribes would move off to the next untouched area to find another supply of food. Often this would involve a two to three day journey. Nothing better demonstrates the effect of modern society than the case of the South Pacific Islanders where diabetes exists at probably one of the highest rates in the world. South Pacific islanders would consume most of the vegetation on one island then all paddle in their canoes to another island which was often a one to two day trip. During this time they had to maintain their energy for the trip, but had little food to consume. The brain does not need insulin to retrieve nutrients, and especially glucose, from the bloodstream. The theory is that the body evolved a mechanism to maintain the brain's supply of glucose at the expense of other organs, such as the muscles, which need a rich supply of insulin for glucose and other nutrients to be taken up by the cells and stored. These hunter-gatherers developed a gene for insulin resistance which is protective. This served them well until the advent of a 20th century lifestyle and the end of a hunter-gatherer society.

The ready availability of food and relative lack of movement due to escalators and elevators, remote control devices, automated transport such as trains, buses, and, of course, our dear friend the car, all affected their lifestyle. Therefore, my friends, the insulin resistance gene is all dressed up with no where to go. What do you expect? No one told the body that life rules were going to drastically change and it hasn't had time as yet to adapt. Although the insulin resistance gene was a wonderful evolutionary device for thousands and thousands of years, in the last 50 years it is very much going against us.

Enter the famous island of Nauru in the South Pacific. A huge 60% of the adult native population of Nauru are non-insulin dependent diabetics. There is only one other aspect of their lives that occurs at a higher rate than non-insulin dependent diabetics and that is the rate of Mercedes ownership. On this famous super-phosphate island the people perform little exercise, drive around in their Mercedes all day and spend most of the day consuming excess amounts of food. They are becoming grossly obese.

Unfortunately, this insulin resistance gene is not only a feature of the South Pacific but occurs commonly in Australian Aborigines, the Maoris, and many people throughout Asia and the Indian sub-continent. The American Indian, and in particular the Pima Indian has the highest rate of diabetes in the world. This condition means that the more affluent people in these areas, and also at times the less affluent, (both groups of which are changing their eating and exercise habits) are developing non-insulin dependent diabetes.

So how does this manifest itself as a disease? Non-insulin dependent diabetes and also insulin dependent diabetes are characterised by two major problems. Firstly, large blood vessel diseases such as coronary artery disease, strokes, aortic anuerysms and peripheral vascular disease (blockages of the blood vessels in the legs); secondly, microvascular disease, or small vessel disease, that is seen commonly with diabetic eye disease, diabetic renal disease and loss of function of the nerve endings in the arms and legs. This second group of small vessel diseases is more common in younger onset insulin dependent diabetics.

Often diabetes only becomes manifest during pregnancy. You will hear terms such as latent diabetes or gestational diabetes. If you do develop a diabetic problem during pregnancy you are definitely diabetic and it is just the extra stress on the body of being pregnant that brings out the diabetes. If you gain weight or have any of the other symptoms mentioned in this chapter it is likely that in later life you will become diabetic.

Despite the form of diabetes present, the mainstay of treatment is not insulin or avoiding sugar but strong attention to all the lifestyle factors mentioned in this book. For example, there is strong evidence now that the use of monounsaturated oils, and in particular olive oil, has a great effect in stabilising diabetes, once ideal body weight has been achieved.

The best treatment for non-insulin diabetes is, of course, weight loss. This is difficult but can be achieved by a motivated patient especially using some of the guidelines in the early chapters of this book. The biggest poisons for the non-insulin dependent and insulin dependent diabetic are saturated fat and cigarette smoke. The trend ten years ago was to suggest diabetics have a low fat, high complex carbohydrate diet but it is now becoming accepted that a low saturated fat, high monounsaturated fat, high antioxidant and complex carbohydrate, ie Mediterranean diet, is the most beneficial for the diabetic. Cessation of smoking and an exercise program are essential. Even a gentle walk daily for a very obese diabetic is better than no activity at all and it has been shown that a stroll through the local town square is enough to slightly improve insulin sensitivity.

I am not trying to suggest that if you follow the lifestyle principles and have significant diabetes that you can throw away your insulin or oral anti-diabetic pills (the so called oral hypoglycemics) but I can promise that if you lose weight and change your lifestyle in the way I have suggested you will achieve much better diabetic control and markedly reduce your chances for the, at times, lethal complications of this condition. There is no point dosing yourself with insulin and falsely believing that this will allow you to overeat. Diabetes is a wonderful example of a condition that, although very much a genetic disease, usually only becomes manifest because of some physical stress. That stress can be excessive amounts of saturated fat leading to obesity and rampant coronary artery disease, cigarette smoking or the pressures of life. If you have already been diagnosed with this condition, I emphasise that following the five point way will keep the diabetes as a benign problem rather than a vicious disease, or markedly reduce your chances of developing diabetes if you are at risk.

Diabetes: Who is at risk?

1. Those with a family history of later onset diabetes.

2. Hypertension — High blood pressure sufferers.
3. Obese people.
4. People with cholesterol problems — especially with elevated triglycerides.
5. Racial background: South Pacific Islanders, Australian Aborigines, Maoris, Indians (sub-continent), South-East Asians and North American Indians.

CHAPTER 6

Don't Feel the Pressure —
Hypertension

When you hear the word hypertension you immediately think of too much stress or pressure. It is only logical because if you break up hypertension into its two main components, 'hyper' and 'tension' this means too much tension, or too much stress. Hypertension, in the medical sense, is elevated blood pressure.

It used to be said that hypertension was anything above systolic blood pressure of 100 plus your age. We now realise this is incorrect. The best definition for hypertension is consistent blood pressure, during the waking hours, of greater than 140 systolic and/or 90 diastolic.

What does this mean? As most of you know, blood pressure is divided into two parts: the systolic pressure and the diastolic pressure. Systolic pressure is related to the force of contraction of the heart. It is, of course, much more complex than this. As we age, blood pressure is affected by the stiffness of our central arteries, especially the aorta which is the main blood vessel of the heart. It is the blood vessel from which all other blood vessels in the body are supplied. The diastolic blood pressure is related to what is happening in the smaller blood vessels. Diastolic blood pressure is an indication of the resting tone in these blood vessels.

We need pressure in our blood vessels to push the blood, and its necessary components, to the tissues but, like everything in life, it all depends on balance. Low blood pressure can be as fatal as high blood pressure.

The higher your blood pressure, the worse off you are. If your blood pressure is normally 100/60 that is better for you than 120/80. Both of these levels are considered to be in the normal range. People who are prone to low blood pressure, have very low rates of heart disease on the whole but also have much greater incidences of fainting and dizziness. Again, it is all about balance.

Say your blood pressure is above 140/90 most of the time? 'So what?' you might ask. The problem is that people who have consistent elevations in blood pressure have much greater rates of heart disease, stroke and kidney disease. These three conditions alone account for over 50% of the deaths in our society. It is therefore vitally important to identify high blood pressure and then to have it treated.

Causes of high blood pressure

It is important to talk about the causes of high blood pressure. If you line up 100 people with high blood pressure and thoroughly investigate them, testing every organ in the body and metabolic parameter, you will find that around 95 to 97 of them have no obvious cause. Obvious causes can be: a blockage or chronic inflammation in the kidneys; a benign tumour of the adrenal gland (the gland that sits on top of the kidney and makes adrenalin and cortisone); obstruction in the aorta which is usually present from birth (known as coarctation); or some other rare glandular disturbance. Such causes only account for 3% to 5%. The younger you present with high blood pressure, the more chance you have of a rare secondary cause.

So what about the 95 to 97 people with no obvious cause? The cause is usually a combination of quite a few metabolic factors. Your metabolism is the way your cells perform their normal functions. You develop your own metabolism from genetics so lovingly given to you by your mother and father, and then the way you live and eat from conception onwards. Every moment, whilst you are asleep, at work, or at leisure, your metabolism is churning away doing the thing it does best — attempting to keep your body in some sort of balance.

Unfortunately, many of our metabolic processes were evolved millions of years ago and are not in tune with our modern lifestyles. Our bodies were geared to be hunter-gatherers and we no longer live like this. The most hunter-gathering behaviour we demonstrate is sending the men out to pick up the takeaway food or the women hunter-gathering our food from supermarkets (I apologise for the sexism). With increased processing and preserving of our foods, we have also changed the balance of the nutrients. There is more salt and less calcium and potassium in the foods we eat and our hunter-gatherer metabolisms are being bombarded with the wrong chemicals.

The end result is an abnormality in salt, calcium and water metabolism. Sodium, potassium, magnesium and calcium are all vital constituents of cell metabolism and are all involved in the messages given to the blood vessels and nerve cells. Calcium is the major cation that directs contraction of our muscle cells. This is not just the muscles we use to lift objects and move our bodies but also the smooth muscle in the lining of blood vessels.

Salt

Excessive sodium in the body leads to the muscle cells being overloaded with salt. The salt draws in water and these muscle cells become waterlogged. If you have the wrong genetic makeup and are exposed to excessive salt and not enough calcium or potassium, then you are set up for high blood pressure.

If someone with a predisposition to high blood pressure is taken out of our society and put into a community where there is almost no salt in the diet, then they will not develop high blood pressure. This, however, is a pipe dream and by the time most of us embark on our hypertensive career, we have already changed our metabolism irreparably and restriction of salt will not really do much to change our blood pressure.

Probably only 20% to 30% of people with high blood pressure will benefit from salt restriction by the time the condition is diagnosed. If one or both of your parents have blood pressure it is better to keep away from the salt shaker. What I advise my patients is:

1. Do not add salt to food on the table.
2. Do not add salt to the cooking.
3. Try to avoid salty food (read labels on packaged food).

If you eat a healthy diet salt is unnecessary to use on the table or in the cooking.

If you are a person who is involved in heavy physical labour in a hot environment then you probably sweat out excessive amounts of salt. You usually know you need extra salt because you suffer bad cramps during these periods of activity.

Note that there is a different form of cramping that tends to occur in older people and this is multi-factorial and really has nothing to do with salt metabolism. If you suffer cramps of this kind, I suggest you seek medical attention and certainly don't start grabbing for the salt shaker.

Diagnosing hypertension

Thirty to 40 years ago, hypertension was a lethal condition that killed people prematurely. If you look back in your family, there are usually one or two relatives who have died of a cerebral haemorrhage or some other nasty complication from high blood pressure. These days, this sort of scenario is less common but I must say the figures for treatment of high blood pressure are still alarming. In the United States it is thought that of the 50% of people diagnosed with high blood pressure only 50% are adequately treated. This means that only 25% of the hypertensive community is receiving adequate treatment.

So what are the answers? Recognition, or diagnosis, and treatment are the answers. At every opportunity, get your blood pressure checked. Every time you go to the doctor take the opportunity to have it checked. If you are found to have high blood pressure get it checked three to four more times. If it is consistently above 140/90 you may then require treatment.

I tend to approach the investigation and treatment of a patient with high blood pressure on an individual basis. If, for example, I have a 45-year-old stressed executive come to see me whose father had high blood pressure and died of a heart attack in his 50s, I would probably not look for a secondary cause (such as a kidney or an adrenal problem) but would certainly perform a thorough screen looking for underlying heart disease. This would include checking cholesterol, triglyceride, HDL, blood sugar, uric acid, the urine for blood and protein, and performing a stress echocardiogram. The point of a stress echocardiogram is to measure the thickness of the walls of the heart, the most important determinant of the severity of high blood pressure and known as left ventricular hypertrophy.

If you have left ventricular hypertrophy, this is the single most important predictor for heart disease and heart attacks.

Vigorous treatment of blood pressure can reverse this process before it becomes dangerous. If I saw a 22-year-old female, who was found on a routine assessment for a job to have high blood pressure with no specific family history of heart disease or blood pressure problems, I would then look for a secondary cause for her condition. Obviously, the treatment of a younger person with high blood pressure is different to an older person. If you do have high blood pressure, you don't have to immediately rush into treatment. Let me say, however, that if you have started on treatment it is, in almost every case, lifelong.

Non-drug therapy

The next issue is whether you should have what we call non-pharmacologic (non-drug) therapy, pharmacologic (drug) therapy or both. The non-pharmacologic therapy is quite useful but usually does not completely control high blood pressure.

I don't know how many times people have come to me and said 'Doctor, I don't want to take pills. What can I do lifestyle-wise to drop my blood pressure?' There are quite a few things you can do but they will probably only drop your blood pressure between 5 mm Hg to 10 mm Hg, both systolic and diastolic. The reality is that we should be aiming, once we have started treatment for blood pressure, to have it consistently lower than 140/90. This doesn't mean that we should be sitting on 140/90 but that we should be aiming for levels of 120 to 130 systolic on 70 to 80 diastolic.

It is important to realise that under times of significant stress, your blood pressure will increase despite all sorts of treatment. One of the most important non-drug therapies to reduce blood pressure is to develop effective ways of dealing with stress. Spend 30 minutes every day in some form of quiet time, anything from sitting quietly in a chair ridding yourself of the day's thoughts and stresses to a more powerful technique such as relaxation therapy and meditation. People who practice daily meditation techniques have less heart disease, cancer and lower blood pressure. Get into the habit of taking this half an hour every day. The first thing you say to me is 'Half an hour, I don't have five minutes every day!' Get up 30 minutes earlier and spend this introduction to the day in quiet time.

Personally, I wake at 5:15 am every morning of the working week and practice transcendental meditation for half an hour before I start my normal daily routine. I find this an extremely effective way of feeling calmer for the day. Sure, I lose half an hour of sleep but it has been shown, in terms of the health benefits and the rejuvenation powers, that half an hour of meditation is probably equivalent to four or five hours of sleep. Other techniques such as yoga, tai-chi, breathing exercises, listening to classical music, or even playing a piano, are wonderful forms of stress release and help keep the blood pressure down.

Regular exercise helps lower the blood pressure and four to five episodes a week of 30 minutes exertion can drop the blood pressure. This also, of course, contributes to weight loss which is another important non-pharmacologic way of controlling blood pressure.

Although salt is one of the central players in the generation of high blood pressure, as I mentioned previously, salt restriction will really only affect 20% to 30% of people with high blood pressure. That doesn't, of course, mean that those of you who are affected by high blood pressure but don't appear to respond to salt restriction, should go crazy with the salt. Salt restriction may not help reduce the high blood pressure but salt excess may be harmful and could possibly raise your blood pressure.

Although the benefits of a low salt diet are often disputed

there is work to suggest that high potassium, high calcium diets help in lowering blood pressure. It would however be irresponsible to suggest an across the board increase in potassium and calcium in the diet. Some people are prone to kidney stones or have other kidney problems and excesses of these two chemicals can be dangerous.

So what about drug treatment? 'But I don't like taking drugs,' you say. Well let me tell you the story of Fritz, one of my European patients. Fritz was 63 and was sick of his general practitioner telling him that he needed to be on drug therapy for his high blood pressure. Fritz stated that any medication affected his thinking ability and the university course he was attempting to complete. I appreciated Fritz's comments but he had seriously high blood pressure and without treatment I knew he was running towards some major catastrophe. His blood pressure was in the 210 to 220/110 to 130 range. I went through the entire list of blood pressure agents and Fritz had a reason why every drug made him sick or upset him in some way.

He had already had a substantial heart attack, had moderately poor heart function, and marked thickening of the heart walls as a consequence of high blood pressure. The combination suggested he was in deep trouble and that his chance of completing his university course was minimal. I tried in the kindest way possible to stress this but he argued with me, stating there must be some alternative treatment for his blood pressure. I gave him the name of a general practitioner who practised complementary medicine. Despite taking herbal preparations prescribed for his blood pressure, Fritz' pressure stayed high.

Six months after my initial consultation with Fritz, he returned to see me and said, 'The reason I am here is to see how fit I am to run in the City to Surf,' (a gruelling 14 kilometre run). I told Fritz that he was more than able to run if he wanted this to be the last event of his life. Fritz left my office disgusted when I suggested he should have yet another try at blood pressure lowering treatment. Four months later, I was saddened but not surprised to hear that Fritz had suffered a cerebral haemorrhage and died a few days later. The unfortunate reality of high pressure is that it is a lethal condition and, without adequate treatment, will shorten your life.

Just to give you some interesting and somewhat alarming statistics, if you have thickened heart walls (no matter what your age) and are left untreated, your risk for a major vascular event (heart attack, stroke or severe angina) over the next five years is around 30%

Drug Therapy

So once we have exhausted all of the non-pharmacologic measures and our blood pressure is still in the 140/90 range what are our next options?

The next option is obviously drugs. These drugs are for life and like all drugs, there are side effects. The unfortunate fact is that if you line up 100 people with high blood pressure and treat them with the one drug, 50 to 60 will be well controlled with minimal side effects and feel quite well. Thirty to 40 will not feel much better and the remaining 10 will have nasty side effects. There is no way of predicting who will suffer the side effects and the trial and error method may have to be used to determine the suitable drug.

There are four main groups of blood pressure treatment and a few other minor groups which are not prescribed as often these days. People who have been on older blood pressure drugs for many years should not be taken off these medications unless they are suffering from long term side effects.

I well remember a man in his 70s who was extremely well controlled on a set of very old drugs. This man had minimal side effects. His normal general practitioner went away on holiday and the practice was taken over by a 'whizz-bang' locum who was up-to-date with all the latest techniques. When the man came in to have his scripts refilled for his blood pressure treatment, the new locum changed him to newer drugs.

One of the very rare but well known side effects of one of these new drugs was kidney failure in people with severe obstruction in their kidneys. This man had been surviving quite well with two major obstructions in both kidneys. This was not adequately checked and his kidneys failed within a few weeks of commencing the new drugs. After he went into kidney failure, it became irreversible. He had a stroke six weeks later and died. There was no reason why this man needed to have his blood pressure treatment changed.

The four main groups of drugs for blood pressure treatment:

1. Diuretics
2. Beta blockers
3. ACE inhibitors
4. Calcium antagonists

The other groups still used are the centrally acting drugs, vasodilating drugs and the other forms of neuronal or nerve blockers.

A few basic comments:

1. One pill will not suit everybody and it may take 2, 3, 4, 5 or 6 different pills before you find one that is suitable.
2. It is better to be on two or three pills at low doses than one pill at a high dose. One of the trends now, especially in the United States, is to combine groups such as calcium antagonists and ACE inhibitors into the one pill.
3. Most people achieve much better control with a once a day pill than taking pills two or three times a day.

4. It is vital that every sufferer of high blood pressure understands the consequences of poor blood pressure control and lack of compliance to medication.

5. Blood pressure treatment is almost always for life. The vast selection of blood pressure treatments these days ensures that almost every person should be able to find a medication, or a combination of medications, that control their blood pressure without causing significant side effects.

Blood pressure in younger people tends to have a different presentation and underlying cause to blood pressure in older people. Older people commonly suffer high blood pressure. What I define as 'old' is: elderly above the age of 70; middle-aged from around 40 to 70; less than 40 is young (but I am getting to the point where I think less than 50 is young). For the purposes of defining high blood pressure, I would say younger people suffering from high blood pressure are less than 55 and older people suffering from high blood pressure are over 55.

A younger person's blood pressure tends to be related to a turning on of their sympathetic nervous system. We have two automatic systems in our body. The sympathetic nervous system is the fear/flight system that makes us jump to readiness when our body is in danger.

The sympathetic nervous system evolved to switch on during periods of heightened activity. It is basically that rush of adrenalin we feel if some idiot almost runs into us on the roads, or our teenage child crashes our car. It is basically the stress system. Younger people who develop high blood pressure tend to have a more sensitive sympathetic nervous system and their heart works faster and harder when they are put under any sort of stress.

A typical person is the hyped-up young executive who comes into the doctor's office and is upset because the doctor is running five minutes behind time. He sits there picking up a magazine, reading the first few lines and then he has to go to the toilet. He is very fidgety.

When he eventually sees the doctor his pulse is running at 95 to 100 beats a minute and his blood pressure is 160/100. He sweats easily and he is worried about this pounding in his chest and feels constantly tired and anxious. These people tend to respond better to drug groups such as the ACE inhibitors or the beta blockers. Both of these drug groups have an effect on reducing the sympathetic nervous system activity.

Older people can experience significant side effects from the beta blockers or the ACE inhibitors. If somebody presents with blood pressure above the age of 55, the underlying causes tend to be constriction in the smaller vessels in the arms and legs, and other muscles, and a stiffening in the major artery, the aorta. These people tend to respond better to the diuretics and calcium antagonists.

The other system is the parasympathetic nervous system. This is the system that is switched on when you are in a deep sleep, to maintain your heart and breathing at its lowest rate. Basically, the parasympathetic nervous system cranks down the metabolism to as low as possible to conserve energy at times when you don't need it. This is the system that signals hunger, commences and facilitates digestion and tells you when your bladder and bowels are full. All of these sensations are completely automatic and, if either our sympathetic or our parasympathetic nervous systems are interrupted by medications or some form of injury, we lose the sensation of these stimuli.

Common side effects from major drug groups

1. Diuretics. High doses of diuretics have been shown to cause problems with metabolism.
   a. Increased cholesterol and triglycerides

b. Increased blood sugar level

c. Increased uric acid levels

d. Drop in potassium and magnesium levels

e. Low sodium levels

f. Fatigue, impotence and skin rash in some cases

2. The beta blockers often cause fatigue, can slow the heart down and can also cause asthma. It is my belief that anyone with a history of asthma as a child or who suffers asthma as an adult, should not be taking beta blockers.

3. Calcium antagonists are divided into 3 different groups. All have the potential to cause swelling of the legs and some can slow the heart down, others can cause headaches and flushing.

4. ACE inhibitors give the symptom of a dry, tickling cough. If you have a cough, go to your doctor to check whether your cough is related to your medication.

Most of the time people do not suffer these side effects and their blood pressure is well controlled by medication.

Each day exciting new advances occur in medical research and the most exciting advance in the field of hypertension is a new drug known as Losartan which is an angiotensin II blocker. This drug has similar properties to ACE inhibitors but does not usually cause the cough which plagues some patients taking the ACE inhibitors. It is just as good a drug at controlling blood pressure and is also very effective for treating heart failure.

A cure for high blood pressure is a long way off. I suspect this cure will come from gene therapy but this may be somewhere between 20 and 50 years away. In the meantime, it is vital that we use a combination of lifestyle changes and medication.

Don't be like Fritz and put your head in the sand. Have your blood pressure checked regularly and if it is consistently elevated, do something about it. I have given you all the ways and means necessary. If it gets to the point in your life where you need to be on therapy, my advice is to accept it. Sometimes we are dealt a bad genetic card but as the famous psychiatrist, Victor Frankl, once said, 'It is not the suffering, it is the way you handle the suffering, that is important.'

CHAPTER 7

Cholesterol

Thirty years ago no one had heard of cholesterol apart from an obscure scientist studying fat metabolism in the back blocks of a university. Over the past 30 years cholesterol has become both villain and superstar, being blamed for almost every illness in the body and being touted as a benign essential substance. Is it an essential substance with limited harmful effects, or a killer relentlessly attacking arteries, blocking them and preventing blood from flowing freely along the tubes?

Over the past 15 years I have been asked many times, 'Doctor, how can I have high cholesterol? I'm thin, I eat the right foods and exercise regularly!' A typical comment is, 'My wife and I have been eating a low cholesterol diet for the past two years and her cholesterol is normal. There must be some mistake with mine!' A real favourite of mine is, 'My friend is 100 kilograms and eats all the wrong foods and his cholesterol is normal'.

Cholesterol is the fat or lipid level in the bloodstream and is determined by what sort of foods you eat, how long you have been dieting, your weight, your genetics and your metabolism. Cholesterol can be found in food or it can be metabolised within the body. It is a steroid like substance that is an essential part of cell structure and metabolism. Without cholesterol in the body an individual would die. The big problem is that the essential level of cholesterol needed in the bloodstream is much lower than the average cholesterol of people who live in affluent societies.

The average cholesterol level is between five and six millimoles per litre. The level of cholesterol necessary for normal cell metabolism is only around two millimoles per litre. Coronary heart disease is almost unheard of in people with a cholesterol level below three millimoles per litre.

Cholesterol and the Generation of Heart Disease

Cholesterol is divided into two major groups. LDL cholesterol is the 'bad' cholesterol and HDL is the 'good' cholesterol. It is quite reasonable to say the more LDL cholesterol, the greater the chance of coronary heart disease, and the more HDL cholesterol the less the chance of coronary heart disease.

A dangerous level of LDL cholesterol is said to be above four millimoles per litre (the lower this level the better). An average level of HDL cholesterol is said to be about one millimole per litre (the higher this level the better).

A low HDL cholesterol (for example less than 1 millimole per litre) even in the presence of a relatively normal LDL cholesterol level, is a very bad sign and carries with it a high chance of the development of coronary heart disease.

When the cholesterol level rises above a certain level, and all the cholesterol necessary for metabolism has been soaked up by the cells, the excess LDL cholesterol moves into the blood vessel system. For LDL cholesterol to cause problems it has to be oxidized. Once oxidized it causes a sequence of reactions within the lining of the blood vessels that have accumulated cholesterol. Initially this causes localized thickenings in the walls of blood vessels and eventually severe blockages leading to angina or a heart attack.

LDL cholesterol appears to be the central player. If the LDL cholesterol is below two coronary heart disease is almost unheard of. Once it is above two there is the possibility of coronary heart disease. LDL cholesterol below four is not completely protective against coronary heart disease. It is important to measure the total cholesterol, the HDL cholesterol and the triglycerides. Triglycerides are another fatty substance that have an intimate relationship with HDL cholesterol.

The function of HDL cholesterol is to act as a scavenger of LDL cholesterol, taking it from the blood vessels back to the liver where the substances are broken down to harmless material. The higher the HDL cholesterol, usually the lower the triglycerides and vice versa.

A triglyceride is a substance made up of three fatty acid groups for each glycerol molecule. They carry a significant amount of fat around the body. For many years they were not thought an important factor in coronary heart disease, but studies performed over the last five to 10 years have highlighted their importance, especially when considered together with cholesterol.

Cholesterol testing

How often should we have our cholesterol levels checked and what tests should be performed? Is a venous blood test or a pin prick test sufficient?

My feeling is that pin prick cholesterol testing is of no real value as it only gives a measure of total cholesterol. Some of the pin prick cholesterol testing machines are not calibrated frequently and often spurious results are obtained. A venous cholesterol sample is a much more accurate test.

Is a venous total cholesterol test suitable when measured alone? I think not. The average total cholesterol in our society is somewhere between five and six and it is essential to have the full picture on total cholesterol, HDL cholesterol and triglycerides.

Approximately 35 years ago, a study in the United States known as the Framingham Heart Study was done in a town 170 kilometres west of Boston. Most of the inhabitants of Framingham were monitored over a period with health aspects such as weight, cholesterol levels, blood pressure, thickening of the heart and other clinical and biochemical factors being checked.

The study found that the average cholesterol level of the residents of Framingham who were admitted to the local hospital with a heart attack was around 6.2 millimoles per litre.

The Framingham study considered all three elements of cholesterol and included a cholesterol:HDL ratio. They found this an excellent predictor for coronary heart disease.

The three components of cholesterol are total cholesterol, HDL cholesterol and the triglycerides. If the cholesterol:HDL ratio is less than 4:5 and the triglycerides are less than 2 millimoles per litre, then the risk of cardiac trouble, such as heart attack or angina, is very low.

The ideal levels should be a cholesterol:HDL ratio less than 3:5 and a triglycerides level less than 1.5 millimoles per litre.

Blood Fat and Cholesterol

What affects blood fat and cholesterol levels?

1. Diet

2. Body weight
3. Length of exposure to fatty foods
4. Genetics
5. Your own intrinsic metabolism (affected by all of the above)

It is not just a simple question of what you eat that determines your cholesterol level. The person who is thin, eats the right foods and exercises regularly may have a significant genetic abnormality which causes high cholesterol levels. It is of no real relevance that a husband and wife may have eaten a low cholesterol diet for two years because the husband may have consumed more despite eating the same type of food as his wife, and because his genetic make-up and intrinsic metabolism will be completely different from his wife's.

The 100 kilogram person who eats the wrong foods and has a normal cholesterol level possibly has an efficient metabolism and may have strong genetics protecting them against the damage of heart disease. Then again, it is relatively common to have a normal total cholesterol level but still suffer from a major heart attack. It is often difficult to separate environmental from genetic factors, as people coming from the same family eat similar foods and have similar dietary habits. The length of exposure to fatty foods and similar genetic make-up will lead to similar metabolisms.

Saturated fat and cholesterol level

Saturated fat consumption has a strong bearing on cholesterol levels. There is a misconception in the general public's mind that saturated fat and cholesterol are one and the same. Cholesterol has a steroid ring and saturated fat is made up of different types of fatty acids in varying combinations. When looking at a patient's risk for coronary disease we consider cholesterol level and saturated fat intake. A 100 kilogram person with normal cholesterol is still in a higher risk group for developing coronary disease because of their saturated fat intake.

Cholesterol Reduction

The cornerstone of cholesterol reduction is, of course, your diet. If diet fails to reduce cholesterol the next step is cholesterol-lowering medications. Ten years ago our options for treatment were relatively limited.

The first available cholesterol lowering medication was a group of compounds known as the bile-acid-binding resins. Binding was a good term because of the effect they had on the gastrointestinal tract. They were effective in lowering cholesterol but produced abdominal cramping (sometimes diarrhoea, sometimes constipation) depending on the bowel. Tolerance to these medicines was low. The average dose was four sachets mixed in orange juice and it tasted like sand. Most people felt they would prefer to take the risk of a major heart attack than spend the rest of their life in the bathroom.

Another medication that has been around for many years, and rocketed into popularity with the help of Robert Kowalski's *Eight Week Cholesterol Cure*, is nicotinic acid or niacin. Nicotinic acid is one of the B group vitamins and when used in high doses has a marked effect on cholesterol and triglycerides reduction and elevation of HDL cholesterol. It is still occasionally used by patients who cannot tolerate other medications.

If taken on an empty stomach (or even on a full stomach) nicotinic acid can cause marked flushing and some preparations have been shown to cause significant liver damage. I strongly suggest that you do not rush out and buy nicotinic acid unless you are supervised by your doctor. A handy hint when taking nicotinic acid is to take an aspirin half an hour before and then take the nicotinic acid in the middle of a meal. I would suggest starting on 250 milligrams (half a tab) twice a day with breakfast and your evening meal.

Gradually increase this to one gram a day in two doses, if this is tolerable. This medication has been shown to contribute to coronary artery regression in quite a few studies and is relatively cheap when compared with the other cholesterol-lowering pills.

Another drug used in cholesterol management was clofibrate. It now has a limited role, having been replaced by gemfibrizol. Clofibrate was effective in reducing blood fats, especially triglycerides, but one study showed a slightly higher incidence of gastrointestinal cancers and a marked increase in gall bladder disease.

Gemfibrizol is a similar drug but has no nasty side effects like clofibrate. It is a very good drug for people with cholesterol problems and especially those with high triglycerides levels. It is a prescription drug and its use should be closely supervised by a doctor.

In the last 10 years a new class of compounds, the statins, have been released. These drugs have a powerful effect on cholesterol reduction and are the world champions at lowering LDL cholesterol. They are very safe drugs with few side effects and are easy to take. You take one pill with your evening meal, but if your cholesterol levels are high two pills may be necessary. The only significant reported side effects from these drugs, apart from skin rash and gastrointestinal upsets, are muscle aches and pains and liver abnormalities. These are rare and can be detected rapidly with a blood test.

Recently there have been some important studies released which indicate that people with or without coronary heart disease may have their lives prolonged by taking the statins. If your cholesterol is elevated and you have known heart disease you should be on these medications. If you do not have heart disease but are in a coronary disease risk group you should probably be taking them.

Two trials reported from the early nineties have been the Scandinavian Simvastatin Survival Study which demonstrated the benefits of taking simvastatin in people with known heart disease, showing a 30% reduction in total mortality and an even higher reduction in cardiovascular mortality.

The other study, from Scotland, known as WOSCOPS and released in November 1995 showed that there was a 22% reduction in coronary death in middle-aged males with high cholesterol but no evidence of heart disease, who took pravastatin, another of the statins. This was the first study of its kind to show a reduction in overall mortality in people without heart disease whose cholesterol was lowered.

Two recent studies of prarachol, known as CARE and LIPID have shown in people with proven heart disease and normal cholesterol levels (4-7 mmol/L) a similar benefit in reducing total mortality, cardiovascular mortality and cardiac events. The interesting finding from these trials was that the benefit was most clearly demonstrated when the LDL cholesterol was reduced below 3.2 mmol/L (115 mg/dL).

Another study that used the oldest of the statins, lovastatin, took a group of 6605 people without evidence of heart disease, average cholesterol levels but low HDL cholesterols.

After five years of the trial there was a 36% decrease in all fatal and non-fatal cardiac events in the people treated with Lovastatin compared to those given placebos.

A new drug known as fluvastatin has been released. It does not appear to have effects on the liver and muscles and has all the benefits of lowering cholesterol. Not only is this drug effective on its own but it can be used with other cholesterol-lowering drugs for people with hard-to-budge cholesterol levels. Sick people with severe kidney failure or organ transplants, whose cholesterol levels need rigid control, can take this drug with little chance of muscle damage.

The most recent statin to be released onto the market is known as atorvastatin. It has the added benefit of significant reductions in triglyceride levels. Like all the statins, its side effect profile is low.

All of these drugs are safe. The three older drugs: simvastatin, pravastatin and lovastatin have proved that the statins prolong life in people with cholesterol problems.

Drugs are effective, but it is important not to relax your diet because you are on medications. An unfortunate habit that has arisen in the United States is for people to take a cholesterol-lowering pill after eating fatty food, believing that this may protect them from the effects of the fat.

There is no substitute for sensible eating. Sensible eating is also not the entire answer and sometimes drugs are needed to adjust your metabolism as well. This is where teamwork between the doctor and the patient is so important for cholesterol and metabolism management.

A frequent misconception is that all people need is a course of cholesterol lowering drugs and their problem is cured. Once you are on cholesterol pills, you are on them for life, in the same way you take blood pressure medication for life.

Cholesterol is not a straightforward issue of reducing your fat or dietary cholesterol intake to solve your problems. It also requires constant dietary planning and management by your doctor.

The new cholesterol-lowering pills have brought about a revolution in the management of fat disorders in the blood, but there is no substitute for a healthy lifestyle.

CHAPTER SEVEN

Determinants of Cholesterol Levels

1. Saturated fat intake
2. Length of exposure to saturated fat
3. Body weight
4. Genetics
5. Metabolism (affected by all of the above)

CHAPTER 8

Vitamins — Fact or Fiction?

If you walk into any chemist shop or supermarket there are shelves and shelves of vitamins and other supplements claiming everything from anti-aging effects to curing haemorrhoids. The vitamin industry is huge and makes some very clever people a mountain of money. What is the reality? Do we need vitamins or is it just a profitable hoax? The reality is that no one really knows!

The fact of the matter is that there have been no controlled clinical studies of any vitamin supplementation in healthy people to prove that taking vitamins will prolong life. In defence of the vitamin industry, there are many traditional medications prescribed that are in constant use and have come through the test of time without controlled clinical trials.

For over 20 years the alternative health movement has been making many claims, for example that vitamin E is helpful in treating or preventing all forms of vascular disease. For over

15 years most orthodox medical practitioners have been saying this is unsubstantiated rubbish.

Well, what are the available facts in the 1990s? We all need a certain amount of vitamins and trace elements to be healthy. The water soluble vitamins, such as vitamin B and C, and some of the trace elements, such as zinc, manganese, and selenium, are essential for biochemical reactions within the body.

Vitamin deficiencies

Without these vitamins, we would develop vitamin deficiency diseases. For example a deficiency of vitamin C leads to the condition scurvy which in the eighteenth century plagued many people on long ocean voyages. A deficiency of thiamine found in vitamin B_1 can lead to the condition beriberi which causes heart failure. A deficiency of niacin found in vitamin B_3 leads to the condition pellagra which is characterized by depression, confusion, dermatitis and diarrhoea. This is quite common in some countries where the population is starving.

Another very common vitamin deficiency seen in our community is B_{12} deficiency, otherwise known as pernicious anaemia. This is in fact not due to lack of B_{12} in the diet, but caused through inability to absorb B_{12} through the bowel because of a long standing gastric problem. Many people are diagnosed as having a B_{12} deficiency purely because they are elderly and feel tired and are given their monthly B_{12} shots in the hope of improving their fatigue.

I have seen patients who were feeling fatigued and improved within seconds to minutes of having their B_{12} shots. When these cases were examined further they did not have any evidence of pernicious anaemia. Lack of B_{12} can give a person a distinctive neurological syndrome where they lose sensation, especially in their legs, and they can become demented.

No one in the medical profession disputes vitamin deficiencies or the importance of having a regular daily intake of adequate vitamins.

A deficiency of the fat soluble vitamins, vitamins A, D, E or K, can have disastrous consequences. A vitamin K deficiency can be associated with major bleeding and some patients can bleed to death. Vitamin D deficiency is closely associated with bone abnormalities and vitamin A deficiency has been linked to night blindness and some forms of bone disease. A lack of vitamin E has not been linked specifically to any disorders. A deficiency of vitamins or a combination of deficiencies can lead to a number of medical conditions that have plagued humans for generations.

With a balanced diet we have adequate amounts of all of these vitamins and unless we have some medical disease such as malabsorption, kidney or liver disease where the vitamins are not absorbed or metabolised properly, we should not need supplements. So the big issue to discuss is whether there are any benefits in the 1990s from supplementing our diet with vitamin pills and potions? It is a staggering fact that 50% of adults in California are taking vitamin supplements of some description.

Antioxidants and cholesterol

When Nobel Prize winning scientist Linus Pauling esteems the value of vitamin C and Lady Cilento, who was well into her nineties when she died, backed up these claims, it makes you think that there may be some basis for vitamin supplements.

Many vitamins and minerals work in the body as antioxidants. The prominent antioxidants are vitamin E, vitamin C, beta-carotene and the other carotenoids, zinc and selenium. Antioxidants protect the body from free radical damage.

85

We only need a certain amount of cholesterol every day for normal metabolism. Once the cholesterol has been utilized by the cells, the remainder of the substance travels around in the bloodstream, looking for blood vessels to block. To invade the lining of blood vessels and cause blockages, it has to be oxidized. When oxidized, by-products are converted into free radicals which can further damage cells. Unless this oxidation process is interrupted, a vicious cycle will be set up. Two major consequences of unrelenting oxidation and free radical release are oxidation of cholesterol and free radical damage to cells, including immune cells. Antioxidants prevent this from happening and assist in preventing atherosclerosis.

For cholesterol to block your arteries, it must be oxidized. Having normal cholesterol levels is no guarantee of safety. If your natural antioxidant mechanisms are not efficient then you run a much higher risk of your cholesterol being oxidized, increasing your chances of progressive and sometimes rapid blocking of the arteries.

Vitamin E and heart disease

Antioxidants (especially vitamin E) form a protective coating around your LDL cholesterol (the bad cholesterol) preventing oxidation from occurring.

People living in areas of the world with high death rates from heart disease (such as Finland and Scotland), medium rates (such as Northern Ireland) or low rates (such as Switzerland, Italy and Crete) were found to have varying blood levels of vitamin C and E. Higher levels were found in the areas with lower heart disease.

The problem with these results is that other lifestyle factors may determine the heart disease rate and the vitamin C and E levels could just be markers rather than the cause.

There have been quite a few studies done where levels of vitamin E, vitamin A, selenium and beta-carotene were evaluated. There is a strong suggestion that the higher blood levels and intake of these chemicals are associated with a lower incidence of heart disease.

Two big studies which have strongly supported vitamin E supplementation were the Nurses Health Study and the Health Professionals Follow Up Study. The Nurses Health Study was a study of 87,000 female nurses aged 34 to 59, who were followed up for approximately eight years. It showed that nurses who took more than 100 units of vitamin E per day had a 41% reduction in their incidence of heart disease.

In the Health Professionals Study, 40,000 men aged 40 to 75 were followed for an average of five years. A 36% reduction in coronary heart disease occurred with vitamin E supplementation.

Over the last few years we have seen a number of reported trials, the most dramatic being the 1996 CHAOS trial (Cambridge Heart Antioxidant Study) which concluded that ingestion of between 400 to 800 units of vitamin E in patients with known heart disease leads to a 77% reduction in further episodes of heart attack.

Recently two other very important studies have contributed to our understanding of how antioxidants work in this setting. The first study comes from the journal of the American College of Cardiology. Around 50 people with proven heart disease were administered antioxidant doses of the above trial of vitamin E, vitamin C and beta carotene in combination, and different parameters in their blood stream were measured including their cholesterol levels and the prevention of oxidation by these three well known antioxidants. The conclusion of this landmark study was that the combination of 800 units of vitamin E, 1000 mg of vitamin C and 24mg of beta carotene significantly reduced the oxidation of LDL cholesterol in people with established heart disease. To put it simply, it is the oxidation of LDL cholesterol (the bad cholesterol) that leads to the clogging of the arteries and heart disease.

The second important study came fron the journal of the American Medical Association in November of 1997 which suggests that if similar doses of vitamin E and vitamin C are taken just prior to the ingestion of a fatty meal then the responsivity of the small blood vessels which control blood flow to the heart and other tissues is markedly improved. Saturated fat in any form is poisonous to our metabolic systems and the ingestion of a fatty meal decreases normal blood flow to organs. It is therefore interesting and gratifying to see these antioxidant vitamins, which have been called useless and expensive, have these important effects.

There are now numerous studies to show that people with higher levels of vitamin E, and those who supplement with between 100 and 500 IU a day, have less incidence of heart attacks and angina. I recommend a daily dose of between 250 and 500 IU of vitamin E.

Beta-carotene and cancer

The most feared complication of free radical cell damage is the generation of cancer. There are now a large number of studies suggesting an association between low levels in the bloodstream of vitamin E, selenium and beta-carotene and the common cancers of the lung, bowel and breast. Lower levels of cancer have been noted in people with a high intake of fruit and vegetables and a low intake of saturated fat.

Studies in the United States, United Kingdom, Japan and Norway are suggesting that where there is a high intake of vegetables rich in beta-carotene, the incidence of cancer is lower. Yellow and orange vegetables such as carrots and pumpkin contain high amounts of beta-carotene. It is thought, though not yet proven, that beta-carotene absorbs free radicals and also boosts the immune system to fight the cancerous cells before they develop.

There is a great deal of evidence to date which is strongly in favour of beta-carotene, vitamin E and selenium helping prevent the common cancers. I suggest a diet high in fruit and vegetables and low in saturated fat. Three recent studies in the *New England Journal of Medicine* did not show any benefit in supplementing with beta-carotene. It is best to get this vitamin from yellow fruit and vegetables, particularly carrots!

Vitamin A

There have been numerous trials regarding the benefits of vitamin A therapy. Vitamin A and its related compounds, the retinoids, have been shown to prevent different types of cancers, especially skin cancers, but I do not support the indiscriminate use of these agents as they are quite toxic to many organ systems in the body, even if taken in moderate doses.

There is increasing work to show that some of the newer antioxidants and other trace elements can have a significant benefit. I am talking of agents such as co-enzyme Q_{10}, selenium and chromium.

Vitamin C

The evidence for vitamin C suggests that doses of between 500 to 1000 milligrams per day facilitate the action of vitamin E as an antioxidant and that it is also a reasonable natural antibiotic. There have been clinical trials that have not supported this view, but certainly there are no studies to suggest any significant harm from this vitamin. I do not support huge doses of vitamin C in the five to 10 grams per day range because I believe all of these antioxidants are like any other drugs — they have therapeutic and toxic levels.

Vitamins - What type?

The reality is (despite the obvious price differences) that most of our vitamins are purchased from the same source and although called natural, do have a synthetic basis. A new concept is to incorporate these synthetic vitamins into baker's yeast, which yields a very concentrated food based vitamin. Rather than the body having to cope with a synthetic substance, the food (in this case baker's yeast) has already performed the physiologic incorporation and this process aids absorption into the body and handling within the liver.

Another new breed of antioxidants are the OPC's. These very strong substances are said to be fifty times more potent than vitamin E. They are derived from either the skin of the red grape or pine-bark. Early results from their use are very promising.

Population Studies

An important way of assessing a treatment or scientific hypotheses is population studies. Although in the assessment of a free living population there are many variables, it is the most natural and least intrusive way of observation. If one nation has a high incidence of heart disease and another has a low incidence, we can can compare all the factors.

We can see whether there are any major differences that could possibly explain why two groups of human beings can have such different disease patterns. This was especially so in the Honolulu Heart Study where Japanese who had moved from Japan to Honolulu, and then to mainland America, had varying and increasing rates of coronary heart disease. The only factor observed in these people was the change in diet that went with these moves. The saturated fat increased as they moved towards America.

Clinical Trials

The major way of assessing the efficacy of treatment or scientific hypotheses is with large scale (or even at times small scale) clinical trials. What happens with a controlled clinical trial is that a large group of the population is studied using some form of medication. The study is supervised by a controlling body and the investigators and the patients are not informed whether they are taking a placebo or the active treatment. This treatment may be anything from a cholesterol lowering pill, a blood pressure pill or a vitamin supplement. The people taking these pills are then followed for a certain period of time depending on the theory being tested. The results of the trial are then published for consideration by the medical profession. Such trials using vitamins have only been carried out in the last decade and not all results have been published.

For many years scientists and practitioners have been claiming that different vitamins can perform wonders for many and varied conditions. There have been those who have said that certain vitamins can cure cancer, including some clinics in Mexico that make somewhat outrageous claims regarding their cure rates. Often these treatments are based around a combination of high dose vitamin treatments, dietary modifications, meditation and massage. More often than not these claims have not been substantiated by clinical trials.

The problem I see with clinical trials is that although people might have relatively similar features in the trials, such as comparable ages, sex, socioeconomic status, disease incidence and so on, there are still many subtle variables that we never mention which can markedly affect the results of the trials.

To give an example, one trial was performed that showed an increased incidence of cancer of the lung in men who had had vasectomies. This was only one trial and it has never been repeated in other trials. So, although there was a statistically significant suggestion that vasectomies could cause lung cancer, it was obviously a spurious finding and should be completely ignored.

There was another study on Finnish smokers where 29,000 smokers were observed for around a 10 year period. Some of these smokers were given beta-carotene, some were give vitamin E and some were given a placebo. The dose of vitamin E was very low (50 IU per day) and not enough to show a strong antioxidant potential. The men did not stop smoking and there was no benefit from taking antioxidant therapy in prevention of lung cancer. A lot of anti-vitamin people saw this study as proof that vitamin E was of no benefit in the treatment of medical conditions. I disagree as the men continued to smoke.

The medical profession uses drugs like cortisone for many and varied conditions, but clinical trials to date have not shown enormous benefits. There is no doubt regarding the harm of cortisone used on a long term basis but this does not stop people using it. I am not against the use of cortisone and have used it on numerous occasions, but feel we should be realistic about the therapy we have available and not dismiss agents like vitamin C just because there are no large scale clinical trials that absolutely prove its effectiveness.

Although clinical trials are useful I do not believe we should base our whole lives on the results but look at the entire picture. Of most importance is the clinical intuition and judge-ment of an excellent doctor who has analysed all the informa-tion.

What is the relevance of this to vitamins? The relevance is that for many years there has been bias in the medical profes-sion against vitamins. I am a great believer in moderation in all things (except, of course, cigarette smoke). This is true when discussing the use of vitamins, or more appropriately, antioxi-dants. If we believed everything the health food people have told us, we could sit down and take between 20 to 30 supple-ments per day with most of our money being spent on these very expensive pills.

We must examine our reasons for wanting to take them. Obviously, it is based around our desire to live longer and live better. I believe that we should draw the line somewhere and take a few well studied, appropriate supplements on a daily basis. Taking vitamin supplements (antioxidants) should never be a substitute for good, healthy eating, but I believe if used judiciously supplements can be a useful part of a balanced lifestyle.

Vitamins — Suggested Doses

1. Vitamin E: 250 — 500 IU per day
2. Vitamin C: 500 — 1000 mg per day
3. Selenium: 50 mcg per day
4. Beta-carotene: eat orange and yellow vegetables
5. Garlic: 440 — 800 mg (powder) per day

CHAPTER 9

Give Yourself a
Sporting Chance

Do we need to exercise or is it a confidence trick set up by
people who own sports stores and gyms? If one looks at the
human body, it is obviously designed for physical activity. The
bone structure and muscle elasticity are designed for movement. Our cardiovascular system works at 10% to 20% of its
maximum rate when we are at rest. The other 80% is for physical activity.

To maintain a lean, trim figure one must exercise regularly.
If you are overweight it is very difficult to lose weight without
a regular exercise programme. But is there any benefit in being
an athlete? Why not be someone who performs just a reasonable level of exercise?

There are no studies to demonstrate that top athletes live any
longer or are any fitter than regular exercisers but there are
many studies to show that people who are overweight or unfit
have more heart disease. A study in the *New England Journal*

of Medicine showed that people who never perform any regular exercise and then suddenly exert themselves have 100 times higher incidence of sudden cardiac death or major cardiac arrests than people who exercise regularly.

There is the occasional person like our Asian businessman who died during exercise, and runner James Fixx who died during a race. This is not the fault of exercise but of the wrong people exercising. Both had symptoms before their deaths.

The 42-year-old businessman who died complained throughout the day of feeling unwell with marked fatigue. Mr Fixx had complained of chest pain for six weeks before his death, but he was told that he was far too fit to have heart disease. It doesn't matter how fit you are, if you rupture plaque in one of your arteries, even if you ran a marathon last week, then there is a strong possibility of a sudden cardiac event.

Squash

It has often been said that squash is a dangerous game and people should avoid it. There was a study done on 22 squash players who dropped dead during the game. Twenty-one of the 22 had commented to either a relative or a doctor in the days or weeks before their death that they had had some chest pain. The problem is not squash as a game, but people with symptoms playing squash. One of the former prime ministers of Australia, Sir William McMahon, played squash until he was 75 years old and he died at the age of 83.

Running

What about becoming a marathon runner? I think not. How many times have you watched television and seen a marathon and cringed at these men or women who are pushing themselves to the limit? How often have you thought how sick and emaciated these people look? Look what happened to James Fixx who wrote *The Complete Book of Running* and died during a race at 49 years of age.

A medical colleague of mine died at the age of 47 following his usual 10 kilometre morning run. Occasionally people have died during marathon runs. It doesn't actually sound like a fun way to die to me.

The reality is, however, that despite the stress on the body, marathon running has a reasonable track record as far as safety is concerned.

A recent study from the journal of the American College of Cardiology examining 50,000 runners participating in successive Boston marathons showed a negligible rate of sudden cardiac death.

There is no benefit (and I believe some harm and risk) from excessive running. Most runners survive their sport, but often people in high risk groups will engage in these excessive body stresses without a correct medical assessment. There is also the risk of ankle, knee and other injuries that occur when pounding the pavement.

If you want to start running marathons and are over 30:

1. Visit your doctor and request a stress test (preferably a stress echo) and a full preventative screen to determine your cardiac risk.

2. Get advice regarding correct footwear.

3. Don't compete if you have had a flu-like illness in the two weeks before a race.

4. If in the days before a race you have symptoms such as marked fatigue, chest pain, shortness of breath or dizziness, consult your doctor immediately and DON'T RUN.

5. If you are a regular long distance runner, consult regularly with a sports medicine physician/physio/trainer regarding stretching exercises to prevent or minimise injuries.

What sort of exercise should we be performing? Is it essential for us to have the colourful leotards or bike pants, a personal trainer and life in the gym with the rest of the sweaty bodies to achieve the goal of super fitness? Fitness is all about moderation. Marathon runners and elite athletes have no health advantages over those who perform regular, moderate exercise.

An article in *The New England Journal of Medicine* around ten years ago examined the psychological profile of marathon runners and found that they shared many of the same characteristics as people with *anorexia nervosa*. It is interesting that many elite female athletes stop menstruating. The intensive training for endurance events can also reduce immunity to infection.

Patients in their forties and fifties have often said to me that they are surprised they have had a heart attack because they

97

were an Olympic rower, or some other high performance athlete, when they were younger. Exercise will only protect you for the time that you spend exercising and within five to six weeks the benefits cease.

Perceived Exertion

Perceived exertion is the feeling you get after two or three minutes moderate exercise when you become slightly short of breath and break out in a light sweat. Once you achieve this feeling you are at approximately 60% to 70% of your predicted maximum heart rate, and it is at this level that you begin burning off fat. To keep fit maintain this exercise for 20 minutes four to five times per week.

This exercise can be any form of aerobics, such as a light jog for half an hour. I say half an hour because it takes approximately five to six minutes of light jogging before you achieve perceived exertion. A game of singles tennis, cycling, swimming, an hour of doubles tennis or even a good, brisk walk will achieve perceived exertion.

You can vary the times of exercise. Fifteen minutes eight to 10 times per week of the same level of activity will give you 10 minutes of perceived exertion on eight occasions. Basically, you need one to two hours per week at the level of perceived exertion and this will keep your weight down and keep you fit from a cardiac viewpoint. Any extra exercise need only be performed purely because you enjoy it.

Get on Your Bike

What about those who detest exercise and believe it is a waste of time? Oscar Wilde said, 'Every time I of think of exercise I go and lie down until the feeling passes'. I see the occasional patients who were never good at sport and always found it a major imposition in their life to exercise. In these situations I try to achieve a trade off: the old exercise bike! Go to the storeroom or garage and dust the cobwebs off the exercise bike and put it in front of your television. It is not particularly aesthetic in the lounge room but it means that every time you walk into the room to watch television the exercise bike is saying to you 'sit on me and pedal for a while'. I believe most people can afford a half an hour per day most days of the week. So switch on your favourite programme, turn up the volume and start pedalling.

Please don't tell me you can't do this or you're not well enough or you're too old. One of my patients was an 88-year-old woman with heart disease induced by blood pressure who had a near cardiac arrest. I recommended a gentle cycling programme on her exercise bike. She watched television and after a few months she would pedal for a good hour and a half and got to approximately 20 kilometres per day. She is still going strong four years later.

Not only is exercise of physical benefit but it also has a psychological benefit. People who exercise regularly find it an amazing stress release. A good brisk walk with your partner, chatting and enjoying the surroundings, can only enhance your fitness and your relationship.

With exercise you must get into a pattern and build up a strong routine, because there is no point going for the occasional run and then not being bothered. It is important to remember that for any behaviour to become habitual you must perform it regularly for at least one month.

Find some form of exercise that you enjoy, because exercise will only do you good for the time you exercise. As soon as you stop the benefit is gone within a few weeks. If you are serious about maintaining a good health programme, exercise has to be an essential part.

Gyms and health spas

Motivation to perform exercise is often lacking. Let's face it, exercise can be hard work and at times can be quite boring. It is important to link exercise with pleasure and many techniques can be used for this.

An excellent form of motivation is joining a local gym. Again, you are exercising with people rather than having to go it alone and specific programs are set out, catering for your limitations and expections. Some people find the one-on-one situation with a personal trainer is much more effective and again a good form of motivation.

One of my patients told me that without a personal trainer he would not bother to exercise because he has no motivation to drag himself to a gym or certainly no motivation to do any exercise by himself. The personal trainer comes to his house and there is no way that he can avoid exercising.

A new concept that has arisen over the last few years is that of the health spa. The health spas provide a comprehensive service not only for exercise, where a gym is available and trainers are present, but also for meditation and all forms of massage therapy, from the gentle Swedish massage to more intensive forms of remedial massage, depending on your needs. This provides a total body service rather than just looking at exercise and will certainly help all aspects of your being, not just the physical.

Some more innovative groups provide a service where you can join a health spa and facilities are available in all major cities throughout the world. This is ideal for the busy traveller who finds it difficult to keep up any sort of exercise program because they are always travelling.This can be quite stressful and by using this facility, exercise can be maintained and stresses can be kept at a minimum. 'Where can I join?'

Exercise — The Essentials

1. Get medically assessed before you begin an exercise programme.
2. Start slowly.
3. Do not exercise when you feel unwell, for example with fatigue, virus, pains in the chest, limbs, abdomen or back.
4. Achieve perceived exertion for at least 20 minutes.
5. Exercise four to five times per week.

CHAPTER 10

The Drinks are on Me

From Teetotaller to Brain Damage

'I've never had a drink in my life!' said my 50-year-old patient, obviously very proud of himself. But is there any health benefit from being a teetotaller?

This question has stirred great debate throughout medical circles and other groups within society. There is a strong anti-alcohol brigade who feel that all alcohol is evil. Then there is the powerful liquor industry which has a vested interest in advertising the benefits of alcohol and playing down its harmful effects.

It has not been shown that moderate drinking is harmful. What is moderate drinking? Most members of the medical profession would say a heavy drinker is someone who drinks more than they do. In reality a moderate drinker is someone who drinks between two to three glasses of alcohol on average per day. The bad news is you can't save all of these up for Friday and Saturday night.

It is interesting to consider the hypocrisy of many medical

organisations: on the one hand they will not publicly support or encourage moderate drinking but on the other hand almost all members of these organisations are regular drinkers, and alcohol is usually freely flowing at their social functions. Remember the German proverb, 'There are more old wine drinkers than old doctors.'

What is a standard alcoholic drink?

An average glass of wine, a small bottle of beer or a nip of spirits is considered one standard drink.

1 glass of wine =125 ml = 1.27 ml alcohol = 10 gm alcohol
1 bottle of beer = 285 ml = 1.27 ml alcohol = 10 gm alcohol
1 nip of spirits = 50 ml = 1.27 ml alcohol = 10 gm of alcohol

How does alcohol affect the body?

There is no doubt that excessive drinking is dangerous. Many lives are lost every year from the ravages of alcohol and many families are destroyed due to the social problems it creates. In the United States alcohol is consumed regularly by about half of the adult population and somewhere between 15 to 20 million people a year are declared alcoholics. Of the 250 million population, alcohol claims 100,000 lives annually and carries an annual price tag of more than one hundred billion dollars. Among persons admitted to general hospitals in America, 20% to 40% have alcohol-related problems.

The liver is the organ most severely affected by alcoholism. In developed countries, cirrhosis is the fourth most common cause of death in people between 25 and 64 years of age. Not only can alcohol cause cirrhosis, but it also causes alcoholic hepatitis, total liver failure, alcohol related diabetes and fatty build-ups within the liver.

Alcohol can cause all sorts of cardiac abnormalities, including rhythm disturbances. It exacerbates hypertension, makes the blood fats go up — especially the triglycerides — and can cause a cardiomyopathy similar to the disease that leads to heart transplants.

The brain is certainly not spared. Alcohol is a direct toxic poison to nerve cells, it can cause dementia, people can lose their balance and can lose sensation in their peripheral nerves. There is generally a higher incidence of cancer in heavy drinkers, especially the upper respiratory tract and the upper parts of the gastrointestinal tract.

What is the basic scientific evidence on the effects of alcohol? Ethyl alcohol, or ethanol, is a source of energy and gram for gram exceeds the energy content of carbohydrates or proteins. There are 29.8 kilojoules per gram of energy for alcohol but only 16.8 kilojoules per gram of energy for carbohydrates and protein, and 37.8 kilojoules per gram of energy for fat.

Once alcohol gets into the body it is metabolised by the enzyme alcohol dehydrogenase to acetaldehyde. Acetaldehyde is a powerful oxidant which can have a profound effect on many chemical systems within the body. Excessive doses of alcohol can generate excessive amounts of acetaldehyde which oxidise many cellular chemicals and do damage to organs in the body.

There are two syndromes caused by alcohol which are not well-known. The first is the induction of a severe behavioural disturbance after only one or two drinks. Affected people can become extremely aggressive and emotional. The biochemical reason for this is not well understood and some lawyers have used this condition as a defence in the case of clients who have committed crimes under the influence of one or two glasses of alcohol.

The second syndrome is associated with a very rare tumour

of the brain. It is known as a pinealoma, which is a tumour of the pineal gland, a tiny organ that sits near the pituitary gland in the brain. The pineal gland controls the release of a substance known as melanin which controls skin pigments. A female with pinealoma can develop alcohol-induced nymphomania, and a small amount of alcohol will set off intense sexual behaviour.

After this discussion on alcohol you are probably tempted never to touch another drink. Let me make the point that the majority of harm done by alcohol occurs in people who regularly consume more than four drinks of alcohol per day.

Studies on Alcohol

It is important to be aware that there are different types of alcohol with different physical effects. In May 1995, the *British Medical Journal* published a study done in Copenhagen. Researchers monitored the drinking habits of 13,000 Danes for around 12 years. There were four main groups.

1. Teetotallers.
2. Spirit drinkers.
3. Beer drinkers.
4. Wine drinkers.

It was found that people who drank three to five nips of spirits per day had 30% more heart disease and cancer than teetotallers. People who drank three to five glasses of beer per day had no benefit, but also no detriment, compared to teetotallers. The staggering statistic was that people who drank three to five glasses of wine per day had 50% less heart disease and cancer compared with teetotallers!

This study was supported by a recent survey from France by well known alcohol researcher Serge Renaud. He found in a study of 36 000 Frenchmen aged between 40 to 65 years, the same 50% reduction in heart disease and cancer only in those men who consumed 250 mls of red wine per day. This was compared to the teetotallers (a group very hard to find in France) and those who drank three glasses or greater per day. After three glasses the rate of cancer and cirrhosis increased with the amount consumed.

My suggestion is that two to three glasses of wine per day for males and one to two glasses per day for females can benefit health. This is where we have to dismiss the concept of alcohol and talk about wine.

The alcoholic drink that is beneficial to the health

As you can see from the studies, not all alcohol has detrimental effects on the body. Wine is a complex mixture of many substances which in small quantities appear to have a good effect on the health. You can extract from apples substances that are poisonous, but in the combination nature designed they are harmless.

The combination of chemicals in wine is in just the right balance to have protective effects on the body. There is a substance in the skin of the red grape known as resveratrol. When the grape is fermented resveratrol becomes a substance known as transresveratrol, which has numerous beneficial effects on the body. Transresveratrol has been shown to reduce LDL cholesterol, and all alcohol stimulates the elevation of HDL cholesterol. In addition red wine contains the three strongest dietary antioxidants we know of:

1. Quercetin
2. Catechin
3. Epicatechin

These three dietary antioxidants switch off 95% of LDL oxidation. Without the oxidation of LDL cholesterol it cannot get into blood vessels and clog them up. This is why antioxidants are important in the diet and the best source is red wine. Two glasses, or 250 millilitres, of red wine per day is all that is necessary for this extraordinary antioxidant effect of switching off all but 5% of the oxidation process. This almost renders LDL cholesterol harmless. Transresveratrol and the natural salicylates in red wine also have the beneficial effect of reducing blood clotting or, in other words, thinning the blood.

The final and very important effect of a couple of glasses of red wine with your evening meal is that it is has a wonderful calming effect and certainly helps to relieve the day's stresses.

I consider white wine to be a weaker version of red, since very similar substances occur in white wine but in much less concentration. If you are a sufferer of asthma and find that the histamines in red wine are overpowering and make your asthma worse, or you have some other allergy-related problem, you may not be able to tolerate red wine and I suggest a glass or two of white wine per day.

To date there have been about 25 studies of the effects of alcohol on humans. They have involved about 600,000 people for five million subject years, and the conclusions are that low-dose alcohol consumption markedly reduces cardiac mortality. Some of these studies have shown that wine consumption has a positive effect on reducing the incidence of cancer.

Like all medications, red wine has a therapeutic and a toxic level. It should not be abused. If you are an alcoholic, or have drunk alcoholically in the past, it is inadvisable for you to use any form of alcohol. Alcohol is a cumulative poison, and if you have had a medical problem or a social problem with alcohol in the past you will reactivate it even with low dose red wine consumption. Only 5% of the population have an alcohol problem, so the other 95% should not be affected.

Alcohol in moderation is acceptable for 95% of us. On that hot day when you want your thirst quenched have a cool glass of beer. The occasional evening finished off with a cognac or a port is also very pleasurable, as long as you don't make this a perpetual life habit. As I have said all through this book, the essence of a long and healthy life is moderation (except in the case of cigarettes). There will always be exceptions to the rule and it is the job of the individual and certainly the medical profession to recognise these exceptions and to deal with them appropriately.

The next time you sit down to a lovely pasta, noodle or rice dish with the ingredients cooked in extra virgin olive oil or peanut oil, you know that when you complement a mouthwatering dish with a couple of glasses of red wine you are not only making the meal taste better but also doing something that can help you live longer.

Red Wine — 2 glasses a day

1. Reduces LDL cholesterol
2. Increases HDL cholesterol
3. Strong antioxidant
4. Natural anti-clotting agent for the blood
5. Relaxant

CHAPTER 11

Clear the Air

Over the last 30 to 40 years there has been mounting scientific evidence about the dangers of cigarette smoking. The number of people smoking has dropped but it is alarming how many people still smoke, especially young people. Young girls are taking up the habit. It is still deemed cool in the teenage world to be a smoker.

Cigarette Poisons

Cigarette smoke contains 48 poisons. The primary poison and main addictive ingredient in cigarettes is nicotine. Nicotine stimulates cellular metabolism, making the cells work harder and faster but not more efficiently. The reason why people who give up smoking put on weight is that their metabolism slows down. The metabolic rate of the body is much higher when smoking.

People who smoke say cigarettes help relax them and calm them down when they are tense. If you are a smoker, when you are under stress of any sort the craving for cigarettes increases. The stress centre and the addictive centre in the brain are close to each other and stimulation of one will stimulate the other. Satisfying your addiction will also satisfy the stress centre and you will have a false sense of calm. To achieve this calm you have to take in a great deal of poison.

Carbon monoxide is a well-known poison found in cigarettes. It is one of the emissions from your car's exhaust pipe. It is as crazy to smoke as to suck on your exhaust pipe. Carbon monoxide damages the lining of the blood vessels predisposing them to coronary heart disease. This lining, endothelium, is an important barrier which protects the blood vessels against damage by cholesterol, sugar and pollutants. Endothelium produces chemicals that open and close blood vessels and protect and repair the lining. If you smoke, the carbon monoxide damages it and blood vessels constrict, affecting blood flow.

Cigarettes contain poisonous benzopyrenes. These are cancer-promoting substances. Benzopyrenes alter the metabolism and function of the cells lining the lungs, and the cells can become cancerous. Recent research also suggests that there may be radioactive matter in cigarettes.

Every time you feel like smoking don't forget you have to accommodate 48 poisons. If one poison doesn't get you the other one probably will. If you want to smoke, remember it has a high probability of killing you.

Who Benefits?

Three groups benefit from cigarette smoking. Doctors see an amazing number of patients with smoking-related illnesses. In 1991 there were two million deaths in the United States. Of these two million, 400,000 were directly attributable to cigarette smoking. Can you imagine the amount of patients doctors would lose if people gave up smoking cigarettes?

The cigarette companies have huge vested interests in smoking and spend millions promoting its glamorous image. But if the cigarette companies tried to introduce cigarettes onto the market these days they would be laughed out of any food and drug administration office for suggesting that such a poisonous substance be made available to the general public.

The third group profiting from smokers is the government, which receives money in tax excise each year from cigarette smoking. It also pays out money on the diseases created by cigarettes. But most cigarette smokers die 10 to 15 years earlier than the rest of the population and the government saves money in the health system.

In relation to other drugs used, such as heroin, cocaine, crack or ecstasy, 80% of drug-related deaths in our society are directly related to cigarette smoking, 17% of deaths are due to alcohol abuse and the other 3% are due to illegal and prescribed drugs.

Addiction

Cigarette smoking is one of the most difficult addictions in the world to kick. Although the level of addiction that affects people is variable, I have seen some patients who are so addicted that, despite having had their carotid arteries (the arteries going to the brain) ripped out, their coronary arteries rebored with coronary artery surgery, their abdominal aortic aneurysm repaired or both their legs removed because of severe peripheral vascular disease, they continue to smoke.

To give up smoking you have to want to. You can attend all the quit smoking programmes available, have hypnotherapy or acupuncture, but if you don't want to stop smoking, you won't. Surgery, scare tactics, propaganda and imminent death are not enough — only personal motivation can get you to quit.

I believe it takes three to six months to work cigarette toxins out of your system. Short term consequences of stopping smoking need to be considered too. Cigarette smoke suppresses mucus production. When a person has been smoking for many years they often produce little mucus and when they stop there is often a reaction by the lungs as the mucous glands 'wake up'. People say they cough more when they stop smoking and they feel sick. Sometimes cigarette smokers will develop an asthmatic illness up to six months after the cessation of smoking. These side effects sometimes drive people back to cigarettes.

Nicotine withdrawal is a real experience and patients can have anything from the obvious craving for nicotine to headaches, irritability and an anxiety syndrome. It is important to persist with quitting and accept these symptoms. Like withdrawal from any addiction there is no easy way, it just takes time.

Diseases from Smoking

Cigarettes are one of the main factors in the generation of coronary heart disease. They can cause coronary artery spasm. People can have normal coronary arteries which at times go into spasm. Eighty percent of people who suffer coronary artery spasm are cigarette smokers. Stopping cigarettes can stop the spasms. Spasm can lead to severe chest pain mimicking a heart attack. Some people have had heart attacks as a consequence of spasm. When their arteries were studied with angiograms they were normal but the heart was damaged by the heart attack from the spasm.

Cigarette smoking is most strongly associated with peripheral vascular disease. Peripheral vascular disease affects blood vessels outside the heart, for example in the legs. This atherosclerosis can initially manifest as pain in the legs during exertion, especially in the calves, thighs or buttocks. When the afflicted person stops walking the pain promptly goes away. To help this condition, stop smoking, begin an exercise programme and take vitamin E.

Cigarette smoking is associated with all other forms of vascular disease such as abdominal aortic aneurysms and stroke. Approximately 60% of cigarette smokers will suffer some form of vascular disease through their lifetime.

Common respiratory diseases are emphysema and chronic bronchitis. The only two significant causes of these are either cigarette smoking or asthma. I don't know how many times I've heard the story of the person who visits a doctor and has a chest x-ray. They've smoked for 20 years and the x-ray says that their heart and lungs are quite normal. They walk away feeling happy about smoking but not knowing a chest x-ray is a very poor way of detecting the cigarette damage.

Do you need to damage around 60% to 70% of your lung tissue before you notice any symptoms? By the time you start to get short of breath it is usually too late. Approximately 60% of smokers will develop chronic airways disease.

The most feared complication of long term smoking is lung cancer. Lung cancer used to be a male disease but as smoking in males has decreased, and the number of women smokers has risen, the incidence of lung cancer in women has increased. Lung cancer is difficult to treat but extremely easy to prevent.

There are many other less common cancers, such as cancer of the lip, upper airways, tongue and throat. There are numerous other conditions that are associated with cigarette smoking. It has an effect on both the liver and the kidneys.

If you smoke, I would strongly advise you to stop immediately. Don't think it's going to be easy and please give yourself six months to get over it. Also realise that because of the effects of smoking on your metabolism, you need to go on a diet and exercise after you stop or you will put on weight.

114

When you stop smoking you will look for something else to satisfy your craving and will probably eat more food. Food tastes so much better than it does when you smoke. There are three very important reasons why you will put on weight when you stop smoking — a change in metabolism, a need for oral gratification, and the fact that food tastes better.

Passive Smoking

Is all the hype from the non-smoking lobby about passive smoking true? Are we dividing our community into the smokers and the non-smokers? Do non-smokers have a right to make smokers feel like lepers if they smoke in front of them?

In January 1990 there was an eight page article in *Circulation*, one of the world's most prestigious cardiology

journals, detailing the hazards of passive smoking. The consensus was that non-smokers who live with smokers for a long time have a 30% higher incidence of cigarette-related diseases than non-smokers who live with non-smokers.

This explains the story I have heard so many times from smokers, my old grandma never smoked a cigarette in her life and died of lung cancer. What they failed to tell me was that old grandma lived with old grandpa who smoked all of his life and old grandma was a passive smoker.

If you want to kill yourself that's your own business but you have absolutely no right to kill anyone else. Passive smoking can increase an adult's risk of heart disease, chronic lung disease and lung cancer, and the children of smokers have a much higher incidence of chronic respiratory illness and infections than the children of non-smokers. I find it bizarre to hear smoking mothers admit they stopped smoking during pregnancy to protect their unborn child but were quite relieved to start smoking at home in the presence of their newborn child.

If you are really serious about your health, make every effort to give up smoking. People do not smoke because they enjoy it, people smoke because they are addicted to nicotine. You can try the nicotine patches, hypnotherapy, acupuncture or quit smoking plans. Please, for your sake and the sake of those around you, stop smoking immediately.

Important Aspects of Cigarette Smoking

1. 48 poisons in one cigarette
2. Nicotine addiction
3. Affects metabolic rate; quitting can cause weight gain
4. Many diseases are related to smoking
5. Passive smoking

Illegal Drugs

There are social and health problems involved in the use of heroin, marijuana, amphetamines, cocaine and ecstasy. The recent death of an Australian schoolgirl after taking ecstasy at a party created public outrage over illegal drugs.

Cigarettes account for 80% of drug-related deaths in society, alcohol for around 17% and all prescribed and illegal drugs account for the other 3%. The greatest drug problems in our society come from cigarettes and alcohol.

This does not mean illegal drugs are harmless and do not create social problems. They are freely available and socially acceptable in drug taking circles. They are expensive and involve criminal activity. Heroin is lethal when an overdose is administered. Needle sharing can transfer HIV and the hepatitis C virus.

A lot of illegal drugs have therapeutic benefits. Marijuana counteracts nausea in people on chemotherapy. Heroin is the best analgesic known. Derivatives of cocaine are used by dentists to dull localized pain. Amphetamines, or speed, are used to treat narcolepsy. These drugs do have a purpose in certain situations but this does not justify their abuse. I do not believe there is any justification for the use of any of these drugs outside a controlled medical environment. The long-term consequences of all drug abuse are disastrous to the user and society.

Marijuana

A significant number of teenagers have tried some form of illegal drug, most commonly marijuana, which is the most widely used illegal drug. Despite what the supporters of marijuana say, THC, the active ingredient in marijuana, is a poison to the body.

CAT scans of the brains of people who have smoked marijuana three to five times a day over ten years have shown a similar degree of cerebral atrophy to brains of people over 70. The younger you start the more sensitive your brain cells are and the more profound the changes will be.

There are three main neurological syndromes caused by marijuana. Loss of short term memory is characterized by not remembering where you put the car keys, or losing your train of thought mid-sentence. You forget what you are doing or your best friend's surname. Psychomotor retardation is having a longer reaction time and tending to perform tasks more slowly than other people. Loss of effective drives is a loss of motivation. The only real motivation marijuana smokers have is to find out where their next joint is coming from. How many times have you seen someone who is a chronic marijuana smoker who has no drive or 'get up and go'.

If you smoke marijuana on a regular basis you have the same chance of developing chronic lung disease as cigarette smokers who smoke 20 cigarettes per day for 20 years.

Marijuana induces hormonal changes in the pituitary gland

and increases the incidence of infertility and the risk of con-genital abnormalities in the children of marijuana smokers, particularly the offspring of males. Just as worrying is the high incidence of acute psychotic reactions and, in particular, schiz-ophrenia, which can occur after the use of marijuana and other illegal substances such as amphetamines.

Marijuana can also cause severe palpitations in people even with only minor cardiac complaints.

Cocaine

Cocaine and the deadly free base cocaine known as crack are highly addictive. One smoke of crack can get most people addicted. People who have used crack describe it as having a cerebral orgasm or the 'ultimate rush'. This momentary rush can cause addicts years of financial and physical misery.

Cocaine is a powerful vasoconstrictor which can cause heart attacks and strokes. A stroke can disable a young person for life.

Heroin

Of all the drugs available heroin is probably the least physical-ly harmful. It is highly addictive, illegal and expensive and addicts will do anything to get their hands on the money for this drug. It is usually injected and users suffer the conse-quences of dirty needles and the possibility of secondary infec-tions, such as hepatitis B and C and HIV.

Heroin addicts are prone to infection of the heart valves, know as endocarditis. This is caused by injecting without ster-ile equipment. A dose of intravenous bacteria hits the heart valves, especially on the right side, and can cause infections which are life-threatening.

Amphetamines

Designer drugs like ecstasy (amphetamine based) are popular at all night dance parties. Amphetamines and ecstasy are used to hype you up so you don't get tired. They are called 'party drugs' because you can dance until dawn with no sleep. These drugs are strong cardiac stimulants and you run the risk of damaging the cardiovascular system, and of addiction.

Drug Culture

For those of us who are concerned about our health it is completely foreign to see how people in the drug culture live. Heroin users will mix up a hit in a toilet using the water from the toilet bowl. Young men and women will sell their bodies in prostitution to get money for heroin, risking sexually transmitted diseases. People share needles, commit crimes and face going to gaol or death as a result of addiction.

Drugs are a form of escape from oneself and life. I believe in almost all cases this is due to a lack of love and a perception of the lack of a future. These are personal and social issues and the problems need to be addressed in the family and in schools, by drug education and the useful employment of people who feel they have no future.

Illegal Drugs

1. Marijuana
2. Cocaine
3. Heroin
4. Amphetamines
5. Hallucinogens

Just Calm Down

Some people find going off to work every day stressful, and when they are relaxing at home, or take a day off, they feel much better. Other people, when they have time off, feel twitchy and edgy because they are not at work. Different people are stressed by different things.

It seems life and work are getting more stressful all the time. This is indicated by the fact that an increasing number of people are taking 'stress leave' from work. Is society becoming more difficult to cope with?

If you live in a large city, you have to be on your guard. When you cross a busy road, the traffic is much heavier than it used to be and there is always the chance of being run over. There is increasing violence in our society. With increased theft security has become big business. Car theft, home robberies and assaults, personal theft of mobile phones, handbags, cameras or designer joggers have put people on their guard in city streets.

On the other hand, life is a lot easier than it was 30 or 50 years ago. Over the past 20 to 30 years we have seen amazing advances in all forms of technology, making our work and play much easier. Entertainment these days is purely a button away on the television or video. The information age of the Internet is at everyone's fingertips. Twenty years ago the computer buffs were the sort of people you would avoid at a party and now they are the flavour of the month. Sitting in front of the computer no longer makes you a social misfit. People involved in computers are now among the most well paid people in society. The richest man in the world is Bill Gates, the owner and creator of Microsoft. But technological advances have not made us happier or decreased our levels of stress.

Better technology raises our living standards and life is allegedly more comfortable. The vicious cycle created is one in which things are more comfortable and more easily accessible so we want more out of life and are less content with what we have. Materialism is replacing human contact. I believe this is mirrored in the fact that many people are turning to drugs and alcohol as a form of escape. The decay of the family and the substitution of a solid, important, long-term relationship with one partner for the quick rush of an affair is a form of escape.

One of the big causes of anxiety and stress is too many choices. The more choices you have, the more anxious you become. Twenty to 30 years ago you could walk into a coffee shop and ask for a cup of coffee. These days you walk into a coffee shop and you are asked whether you want cappuccino, espresso, flat white, short black, long black, or a de-caf with a twist of lemon. Do you want milk? Is it skim milk, low fat milk, substitute milk, soya milk or goat milk? Do want sugar, honey or saccharine? Tea is a choice between Liptons, Darjeeling, English breakfast, Earl Grey, Prince of Wales or herbal. We have too many choices.

When we look at relationships, it's no longer falling in love and getting married. It's falling in love with a choice of sexes, living together or living apart, monogamy or multiple partners, safe sex or unsafe sex? Do you want to be homosexual, hetero-sexual, bisexual or asexual?

In a world where a peasant working in the fields develops an illness and is told that he has six months to live, when asked how he wants to spend the last six months he knows that he has no choice. He will continue to work in the fields and die when it is his time to die. When you pose a rich Westerner the same problem, he wants to experience almost everything there is to experience in that short period of time. He has more choices than the peasant.

Our life revolves around three activities

1. Work
2. Leisure
3. Sleep.

A problem with either your work, leisure or sleep will lead to a feeling of anxiety or depression. If one of these aspects of your life is upset it will flow into the other areas. Often people who are successful at work spend far too many hours in their day maintaining that success and reduce the amount of time they have to play.

Work

Many people I know in my profession have sacrificed their lives to work, seeking positions or doing medical research, and totally neglecting their personal lives, to the detriment of their families. Although they have the respect of their peers, they do not have the respect of their families. They are successful in one aspect of their lives. I believe to be a total success you should try and achieve a balance between work, rest and play.

123

We are expected to put a supreme effort into work between the ages of 25 and 55, the very time that our families, and especially our children, need us the most. We often spend between eight to 10 hours per day working. This accounts for almost a third of our adult life. It is important to enjoy yourself. There is no point fronting up for work every day feeling totally miserable, watching the clock and hanging out for that two to three week holiday at the end of the year.

The Boss

At work you are either the boss or an employee. If you are the boss you are in control, earn more than your employees and carry most of the responsibility. If it is your business, you are responsible for the quality of the service provided. You are in a position of authority and carry the responsibility, status, extra worry and, you hope, extra income that goes with this position. You must take pride in the quality of the service your particular business provides. This will reward you personally.

If you only look at the financial result, you'll feel the constant pressure of earning money and lose sight of the real essence of life, which is service. One of the great stress relievers is the feeling of satisfaction that you are delivering a good service, not the feeling of satisfaction that the dollars are rolling in. People who want a lot of money are hard to satisfy.

If the primary aim of your business is to provide an excellent service then your stress levels will be reduced. This can begin with the quality of service you give your employees. If your employees know that you care about them (not just giving superficial lip service) they will be more inclined to give 100% to the business.

Mistakes are made. Point out the mistake, even show some degree of displeasure, and then forget about it and get back to work rather than making the person involved feel bad by bringing it up again and again. This is counterproductive, leads to disharmony and tension in the workplace and increases stress.

How the workplace functions is often dependent on how the boss runs the show. There is an old joke, 'there's nothing wrong with school, it's just the principal of the thing'. If your business is an unhappy place, it is your fault. You selected the employees, you own the business and you have the power to do something about it. Choose the right people for the right jobs. This will decrease your day-to-day stress.

I knew one fellow who was so rude to his staff that he went through one secretary a month. He could never understand why people kept leaving him and could not understand why people wouldn't give him good service. He had no insight into his personality.

The Employer's Check List
1. When was the last time you asked your staff how they enjoyed their weekend?
2. When was the last time you complimented a member of your staff about a job well done, his or her appearance or ideas? When was the last time you showed some interest in your staff as people?
3. Do you take them out to lunch occasionally?
4. Do they call you by your first name? The boss should be in charge but not be aloof and unapproachable.

Five Factors Affecting Work Stress
1. Personal relationships at work
2. Office design
3. Extracurricular activities
4. Health assessment and management
5. Remuneration

1. Personal Relationships

As an employee you should value your position and feel valuable. The manner you use on the phone, in dealing with the customers and your workmates is important to maintaining quality of service and workplace harmony. Recognise that you put in your best effort whether you are the boss or an employee. Working together with consideration and communication is vital. Personal relationships at work are based on respect.

2. Office Design

The design of the office is important. To work in an office with no windows, fresh air or natural light can have an adverse effect on people's health and well-being.

Sunlight in the interior of the office is important to maintain a calm and relaxed atmosphere. Plants and flowers add life. Decor and paintings are influential. People will be more productive and alert if their desks have a reasonable view.

It is better to get out at lunchtime than sit in a staffroom. Even a ten minute walk can clear the head. Try not to work during your lunch break. Practise a relaxation technique, meditation or simple yoga in your break.

3. Extracurricular Activities

Conferences and courses to improve skills are important to maintain enthusiasm and keep your office techniques and methods up-to-date. They also stimulate work production and interest.

4. Health Assessments and Management

For large corporations with people working under tremendous pressure, it is important that the health of the staff is assessed and cared for. This involves the right education in areas such as eating, exercise and stress management. I believe preventa-

tive strategies and good health assessments can add 10 to 15 extra years of quality life for those of us working under pressure.

The needs of a 25-year-old secretary are completely different from those of a 48-year-old executive manager with a mild elevation in his blood pressure and cholesterol. All of these issues should be addressed by an expert in the area.

5. Remuneration

Someone working in a difficult and high pressure job should be paid appropriately. This important aspect is often lost in the maze of employment but if you pay peanuts you get monkeys.

Leisure

The most successful people in society have not only an interesting, satisfying and well paid job but manage to combine this with an equally satisfying, enjoyable and, I hope, passionate leisure time.

The most important aspect of life in making people feel complete is loving relationships with people. If you have a defective relationship with your partner this will have a profound effect on other aspects of your life. There is no point climbing your way up the ladder to success and neglecting your partner in the meantime. You should put even more effort into this relationship than you do into your work. Your work may take more hours in the day than your relationship, but a strong supportive relationship can get you through any one of life's crises.

Talk to each other. Spend a portion of each day sitting down together over dinner, or after dinner, with a glass of wine. Be interested in your partner's daily activities and be sensitive to his or her needs. Have time alone, away from other people, including your children. I would suggest that at least one to two weekends a year you should make time to have a few nights away with your partner. To get away from your environment and routines adds a new dimension to your relationship.

Another important part of your leisure time is your relationship with your children, if you have them. It has only been in the last 10 to 15 years that those of us dealing with the psychological aspects of human behaviour have realised the profound effects of parenting, especially in the first five to 10 years.

A baby is a clean slate, and every experience from the uterus to starting school lays down the basic foundation for behavioural patterns for the remainder of that person's life. I have often heard people say, 'My father was a great success at his job but we never saw him.' No matter how busy you are, try to fit in time for your children. Try to read to them at night and talk with them and listen to what they have to say.

Be there for your teenagers and realise no matter how difficult they may seem, they are purely testing you and desperately crying out for boundaries and discipline. It is very important for those boundaries to be put in place. They will rebel but they still need to know that their parents care for and love them.

It is important to have a wide circle of friends outside your family. Other people you know enjoy your company and depend on you for friendship, caring and occasional favours. Keep in touch with them — don't expect them always to be ringing you. Relationships of any sort work both ways.

Sport is an excellent way to spend your leisure time. Playing team sport encourages good socialising and a sense of friendship. In most sports there is to some degree a breaking-down of social barriers, and this gives you a better understanding of people.

I believe every one of us needs at least half an hour each day to withdraw from our responsibilities and our contact with others. Religious people achieve this beautifully with prayer. It can be listening to a relaxing piece of music or sitting in the garden sipping a drink. I achieve this 'time-out' with daily meditation. There are now many meditation courses available and the stress release from this daily practice is huge.

A regular massage keeps the muscles toned and is also a wonderful stress reliever. Have it first thing in the morning when you and the masseur are fresh.

Sleep

If we divide our life into thirds, we spend around eight hours a day working, around eight hours a day in leisure activities and around eight hours a day sleeping. This varies with the individual. Sleeping rejuvenates us. The very deep sleep, when we are dreaming, is the most beneficial.

We need less sleep as we get older. A newborn baby sleeps for around 23 hours per day and as children develop through their early childhood years to become teenagers their need for sleep reduces. Once you become an adult you need around six to eight hours of sleep per day. When you are in your seventies or eighties you may only need three to five hours sleep a night as you often have less to do than in the years from the twenties to the fifties. Discover exactly how many hours of sleep you need to feel refreshed when you wake and sleep that amount of time. There is no point getting up too early if you are going to feel tired throughout the day.

Sleeping tablets do not help you sleep. Sleeping tablets are sedatives that give you a false sleep and increase sleep apnea. I believe the only place for sleeping tablets is in situations where people are under an acute stress and are getting absolutely no sleep, or in unusual circumstances such as long plane trips. There are so many other techniques available to improve your sleep that it is unnecessary to use artificial means. One important technique is to avoid any stimulants prior to going to bed. If you are foolish enough to have a cup of coffee or a strong cup of tea before bedtime you will pay the price by finding it hard to sleep. The same goes for Coca Cola and chocolate. Try not to go to sleep on an argument. Arguing with your partner prior to sleeping will obviously keep you awake.

Don't take your work to bed. Lying in bed worrying will only keep you awake. Read a little before to going to sleep. It should be enough to just push you off to sleep.

The most natural sleep-inducer known to humans is a good orgasm. If you sleep with someone you love, love-making before sleep allows you to have an extremely good night's rest.

If you find it very difficult to get off to sleep or continually wake during the night, there are quite a few other effective techniques to help you sleep. There is a vast array of subliminal sleep tapes on the market. Progressive muscular relaxation is also a good method of physical relaxation. Lie on your back and relax each muscle group, starting with the right leg going to the left leg, right arm, left arm, abdomen, through the back, up the neck, scalp and then the face. This technique can also be used when you wake in the night.

If you are waking throughout the night you must look at the reasons. You may have a medical problem, such as a urinary infection or kidney disease which makes you get up frequently to pass water. There are other conditions such as restless legs syndrome or cramps which can be treated by a doctor.

Four Causes of Tiredness

Stress
A cause of tiredness in our society is stress. People with stress at work, stress at home or ineffectual sleep will feel tired.

Depression

The next most common cause of tiredness is depression. There are many misconceptions regarding depression. People will often say that a person is depressed because his life is going badly, but it is often the case that the person's life is going badly because he is depressed. There are two basic types of depression. Reactive depression can be set off if a loved one dies, you have been sacked from a job or you have an acute physical illness that takes away your enjoyment of life. To feel depressed is a normal response to an abnormal situation.

Endogenous depression is a chemical depression just like diabetes, Parkinson's disease or thyroid disease. Chemical depression affects the brain but no other organs. It may be precipitated by a life event, but is more commonly precipitated by an acute physical event, such as a severe virus, an episode of pneumonia or coronary artery bypass surgery.

A famous entrepreneur was thought to have memory loss after bypass surgery. It is more likely that he suffered a depressive illness, common after coronary artery bypass grafting.

I remember one patient I saw who had had coronary artery bypass grafting five years before. He said to me, 'Doctor, my angina is cured but I have felt lousy ever since my surgery.' I put him on a course of antidepressants and within six weeks he was back to his old self and feeling marvellous.

The problem is that antidepressants are often prescribed inappropriately and are given to people with reactive depression and not endogenous depression. You cannot pull yourself out of endogenous depression. There are only three possible treatments. One is antidepressants, the second is electroconvulsive therapy (electric shock treatment) for people who are severely depressed and the third is time.

All the counselling in the world and support from the family will not help. Severe endogenous depression is a dangerous condition, killing around one in six people who are affected by it. They often commit suicide and at times will take members of their family with them. They feel that life is so bad for them it must be bad for their loved ones and they try to put everyone out of their misery.

Symptoms of endogenous depression are altered sleep patterns (waking very early in the morning and not getting back to sleep), loss of appetite, weight loss, not feeling a zest for life, inappropriate emotional outbursts and a feeling of sadness. The main symptom of endogenous depression is tiredness.

Sleep Apnea
This condition is relatively common and all adult males will suffer sleep apnea at some stage in their life, especially after a heavy night on the booze. What basically happens in sleep apnea is that the upper airway closes off when one drifts into a deep sleep. You will be aware of the sleep apnea sufferer. This is the person who is moderately to extremely overweight, smokes and drinks to excess and is a heavy snorer. He is the kind of snorer the neighbours complain about.

These people snore and snort and choke throughout the night. As they are going into deep sleep they close off their airway. This causes them to almost wake and they return to a lighter phase of sleep, starting the process all over again. The person never has a deep sleep and feels constantly tired during the day. Always tired, they fall asleep while they are driving. They fall asleep in front of the television within seconds and often fall asleep in company.

Sleep apnea can be treated with a mask known as a nasal C-PAP mask. It is fitted over the nose and maintains positive air pressure in the back of the throat, keeping the airway open during sleep. About one in 20 people find it difficult to tolerate the mask but most people benefit and can have a proper sleep. The morning after a very heavy night on alcohol, when you feel dreadfully hung-over and very tired, is due to the toxins in the alcohol and sleep apnea. Women usually do not suffer from sleep apnea until menopause, and then they have the same incidence as men.

The way to avoid sleep apnea is simple:
1. Reduce your alcohol
2. Stop smoking
3. Lose weight
4. Develop a proper sleeping habit

An Underlying Medical Illness
Some illnesses such as influenza are obvious, but some are less obvious such as anaemia, thyroid disease, undiagnosed heart disease and cancer. It is important if you feel chronically tired to be assessed by your doctor.

If you have an underlying condition your energy levels during the day are markedly affected. I often see patients with severe heart disease who are relatively well for a couple of hours during the day but then become tired and have to rest. They expend what little energy they have in a very short period of time.

A wise physician, who was the man who inspired me to do cardiology, Dr Don Anderson (one of the founders of the Australian National Heart Foundation), once told me that patients with a severe heart condition should spend a day in bed every week to rejuvenate themselves. I don't know how many times I have heard patients say they felt fine for a few days after a day's rest, but after a busy day had to go back to bed for a day to recuperate. I believe this is to do with expenditure of limited energy reserves.

It is vitally important that all areas of your life — work, leisure and sleep — are cared for. If your life is unbalanced you set yourself up for either a physical or psychological breakdown and you will miss out on the great richness of life.

Causes of Stress

1. Modern life
2. Work
3. Leisure
4. Sleep
5. Tiredness

CHAPTER 14

Give Me Five

In this book I have tried to present a commonsense, moderate approach to a long and healthy life. Not only have I presented a cardiologist's point of view on how to keep your heart healthy but I have also presented the wholistic approach. In my career I have tried to use a combination of the best orthodox medical techniques and what I consider to be the useful parts of the so-called alternative medical therapies. This is an introductory guide to the important preventative strategies for maintaining a healthy life.

So what about our Asian businessman, why did he die so suddenly? The fact is that he had been feeling unwell all day. Unfortunately this was not recognized and he died during exercise. What happened to him was due to his family history. His father had died at around the same age of the same condition, developing exactly the same problem. Despite the fact that the businessman did not smoke, exercised and ate all the right foods, he was working in a very stressful position and had dreadful genetics. I suspect that he had a cholesterol problem because of his genetics and that this generated coronary heart disease. On the day of his death, or possibly beforehand, he would have ruptured one of his fatty blockages. His symptoms on the day of his death were due to the progression of the blockage, with bleeding into the wall of the artery, and a clot forming over the top of the blockage. This closed the artery completely and caused a massive heart attack.

Why didn't our 53-year-old pilot experience any symptoms, despite having severe coronary heart disease? Every person is different. Some people have very high pain thresholds, some people have very low pain thresholds. Some people proudly boast that they can tolerate pain but this often masks significant underlying problems. Our pilot had a very high pain threshold and so may you. All the more reason why you should not only follow the lifestyle suggested in this book but have a regular checkup with your doctor, especially if there is some known risk for heart disease or cancer.

What about Mr Fixx? Doesn't marathon running make you immune to coronary heart disease? Of course it doesn't and it never will. For six weeks before his death Mr Fixx had symptoms that went undiagnosed. Had they been recognized he would have been able to have appropriate treatment, and would have been advised not to exercise until the problems were sorted out. His life may have been saved by a correct diagnosis.

What about the 50 year old heart surgeon. How could he have such a high calcium score on Electron Beam Tomography without any warning symptoms or major abnormalities on other tests such as Stress Echo and Coronary Angiography?

One of the problems with coronary heart disease is no warning signs. One third of people will die before they make it to the hospital with their first presentation of coronary heart disease. Death is a drastic way to get attention.

137

All the major risk factors such as high cholesterol, cigarette smoking and high blood pressure only account for around 50 per cent of coronary heart disease cases. In Daniel's case he had excesses of an abnormal chemical in his blood stream known as lipoprotein (a) or Lp(a), which led to significant fat build up in the lining of his arteries without as yet causing obstruction within the lumen. The only way to control this chemical is with aggressive cholesterol lowering therapy, intensive antioxidant treatment and a lifestyle transplant. Without proper lifestyle change and medical treatment, the fat within the wall of Daniel's arteries could rupture into the lumen possibly leading to a major heart attack. Scientists are trying to find a drug or genetic treatment that will reduce lipoprotein (a) levels but as yet none has been found. The bad news is that this condition is not rare. One in five people in Western society have excess levels and almost all go unrecognised, their premature heart disease being explained as bad luck.

Why does our construction worker survive despite a less than perfect lifestyle? Basically because there are occasional people who are genetically well-disposed. Our genes will often determine what sort of diseases we will have in our lifetime. Our lifestyle will often determine when we develop those diseases. Every now and then someone comes along, like our construction worker, whose genetic constitution is so strong that self-abuse poses no significant threat to him, but don't take this as an excuse to abuse yourself if both your parents lived into their eighties!

The message is very clear: to give yourself the best possible chance of a long and healthy life you should combine important lifestyle management with medical care.